Stamp Collecting

COLLINS NUTSHELL BOOKS

Stamp Collecting

E. H. SPIRE

With Photographs and Line Drawings

COLLINS
LONDON AND GLASGOW

GENERAL EDITOR: J. B. FOREMAN, M.A.

First published, 1962
Revised edition, 1970

Contents

ACKNOWLEDGMENTS

The publishers are very grateful to Messrs. ROBSON LOWE, LTD., of London, who co-operated so willingly and lent all the colour blocks.

List of Photographs

CHAPTER I

Introduction to Philately

Stamp collecting is the most popular hobby in the world. Yet, to some people it may seem like a waste of time, effort and money to accumulate a lot of " tiny pieces of coloured paper," stick them into albums and pore over them with a magnifying glass for hours on end. Why then do millions of people collect stamps, not only in their childhood but throughout their lives, and why is the hobby recruiting every year at least three million new enthusiasts?

Stamps have often been described as the visiting cards of nations. In many ways they reflect the history of their countries, convey the sensation of travel to far-away places, depict strange landscapes, tell of the customs of many races. Many stamp designs portray famous men and women, inform of historical events and of the progress of science, and instruct about art and architecture.

President Franklin D. Roosevelt, an enthusiastic, life-long collector, put it perhaps most clearly why stamp collecting is of particular value and interest:

" The best thing about stamp collecting as a pursuit is that the enthusiasm aroused in youth increases as the years pass. Stamp collecting dispels boredom, broadens our knowledge of lands and peoples, and in innumerable ways enriches life and adds to its joy."

Those who have been bitten by the collecting bug will certainly agree that their hobby is the most interesting any man, woman or child can take up.

No one can say for certain when stamp collecting

began. It is said to have started in a boys' school in Paris, when one of the teachers encouraged his pupils to stick any foreign stamps they could obtain in their atlases, on the back of the map of each country, in order to render the study of geography more interesting. This may be so, but it is also certain that only ten years after the first postage stamp, the " Penny Black " of Great Britain, had appeared, there was a handful of eager collectors. From then on, like Topsy, it just " growed," and was there before anybody had noticed its birth. It has been growing ever since, until to-day the number of serious collectors in the world is estimated to exceed thirty million.

No other hobby, game or recreation, including cricket and golf, can boast such huge legions of active amateurs. Admittedly, stamp collectors were at first looked upon as cranks and their hobby as suitable only for schoolboys. Nobody believed then that the craze would last more than a few years and, indeed, many people declared that the experiment of sticking little labels on letters as a means of pre-paying the postal charges was doomed to failure anyway.

But stamps have now been with us for more than a century and, even after the advent of automatic franking machines which large business firms use and which indicate by a printed mark the payment of postage and the date of posting, the overwhelming bulk of daily correspondence still bears adhesive postage stamps.

Over the century since the invention of postage stamps, stamp collecting has developed into the science of philately (from the Greek words *philos*, loving, and *ateleia*, exemption from tax or payment). Moreover, the hobby has created a big business and an industry with world-wide ramifications, giving employment to many thousands of people in dealers' shops, album factories, auction rooms, publishing companies and editorial offices. Many governments welcome the hobby as a profitable source of state revenue and, indeed, the budgets of some small countries are balanced to a large degree by the issue of new, attractive stamp series.

The astonishing financial ramifications of stamp collecting are described in a later chapter, but I may mention here that hundreds of millions of pounds are tied up in dealers' stock and invested in valuable collections, and that between £15,000,000 and £20,000,000 is spent or turned over on stamps every year in Great Britain alone.

The beginner at stamp collecting has to buy his experience and inevitably makes mistakes. The opportunities for picking up fantastic bargains such as came the way of the earliest collectors are few and far between. But for the true amateur the financial side of his hobby will always seem of secondary importance. The value of his stamp collection will give him confidence in spending money on his hobby without fear that it will be wasted, but what will really interest him will be the enlarging of his collection and the acquisition of as many interesting items as possible for the study of them, even if many of them are quite common stamps.

There are several ways in which the beginner can accumulate the nucleus of his first collection of stamps. The most economical is undoubtedly to persuade a friend or relative, who collected stamps in his or her youth and, for some reason, has long since lost interest in the hobby, to make a gift of the forgotten, tucked-away album. But in these days this happy method is rarely successful. For one thing, the friend or relative taking the album out of the drawer or trunk will only too often be fired to start collecting anew; and for another, most owners of old collections will realise their value and will be reluctant to part with them.

The widespread belief that a good collection can be built up by asking family friends for the foreign stamps from their correspondence is unjustified optimism. Certainly, the beginner should tell all his relatives and friends of his new hobby and he may sometimes be presented with a few stamps, but it is a slow and chancy method. Most of these stamps will be similar, common, and current specimens. All the new philatelist will accumulate will be a pile of duplicates.

The first question the beginner should ask himself is whether he wants to become a " general collector," or to concentrate on the stamps of a group of countries or a continent—for instance Britain and the British Commonwealth, or Europe, or U.S.A. In spite of the ever increasing trend towards " specialisation," caused by the huge numbers of new stamps issued every year, I advise the newcomer to philately to start as a " general collector," i.e. to collect stamps from all over the world. This will give him, for the first few months at least, a wider knowledge of stamps, enhance his knowledge of history and geography, and provide more pleasure.

After a time even the raw beginner will decide to limit his scope to a number of selected countries. This will enable him to concentrate his further study of stamps and, perhaps, encourage him to embark later on some sort of " specialisation."

No large outlay of money is necessary at the beginning. The cheapest and easiest way to start a collection is to buy a large packet of " world mixture," containing 1,000 or 2,000 stamps, which dealers offer at prices of between 30/- and £3. Such " world mixtures " comprise stamps from thirty or more countries, usually including many attractive pictorials.

On many evenings and holidays the happy owner will be kept busy sorting out the stamps, getting order out of chaos, discovering new countries, learning to recognise puzzling items, getting acquainted with stamp designs, denominations, watermarks, perforations—in short, acquiring an idea about philately as a whole. He will be learning the game.

Many dealers send out booklets with stamps " on approval." Each item is priced, and the collector can pick stamps he desires to buy and return the remainder, enclosing his remittance for the stamps purchased. Some dealers offer " free gifts," but as no trader will give something for nothing, one can be sure that the value of the " free " gift has been carefully included in the price of the stamps offered on approval. There are, as in every trade, reliable and less reliable sources of supply. The beginner will be well advised to carry his custom to one of the many reputable dealers.

It might be a good idea to make a " finance plan," deciding to spend so much every month on the new hobby. This will enable the beginner to acquire stamps regularly and later, perhaps, to join one of the " new issue services " run by many dealers. He may also visit auction rooms where often a good bargain can be acquired by bidding for a general collection or a " remainder " in an album. If he spends too much money at one go, he might be prevented from buying stamps for a long time and this may well discourage him from continuing his hobby.

To find the addresses of reputable dealers and also to get the first glimpse of philatelic reading, the beginner should, from the very outset, subscribe to one of the philatelic journals. If he does not wish to pay a subscription, most of them are also sold in stamp dealers' shops, at bookstalls on railway stations, and by many newsagents.

Later on the beginner will find out whether there is a philatelic society in his home town or district and apply

13

for membership. The annual subscription is usually only a few shillings and well worth it. At club meetings the beginner will not only meet many knowledgeable philatelists who will be pleased to assist and guide him, but he will be able to attend displays and lectures on many philatelic subjects and take part in the " Exchange Packet " and in club auctions. When he has accumulated a fair number of duplicates he will attempt to " swop " them for stamps offered by other members. Some of the great advantages of membership of a philatelic society are described in Chapter 14.

Within a few weeks and without really realising it, the new recruit will become a fully-fledged stamp collector, although it will take quite a few years before, by assiduous study, he will be able to describe himself as a serious philatelist.

CHAPTER 2

An Outline of Postal History

The history of postal communications is as old as that of our civilisation. In ancient Egypt, under the twelfth dynasty, 1500 years before Christ, runners carried letters written on cuneiform tablets. The Israelites had a messenger system nearly a thousand years before Christ's birth and when Cyrus the Great founded, around 540 B.C., the Persian Empire which extended from the Himalayas to the Mediterranean and from the Caucasus to the Indian Ocean, he relied on the *angaros*—mounted couriers—for communication with his satraps and governors. The Greek states had a postal system of sorts which greatly expanded with the Greek colonisation of the Mediterranean.

The Romans brought the ancient postal system to perfection by creating a corps of mail runners, the *cursores* and *tabellarii* (from *tabella*, small clay tablets) and later a relay service by mounted messengers, the *cursus publicus*, which connected Rome with its great Empire.

After the fall of Rome, the mail services, used almost exclusively for official and military purposes, declined in Europe. It was not until the 14th century that something like organised postal communications were established, particularly in France and in the German free cities.

The development of a postal service in Britain can be traced to the horsemen who carried despatches for the Tudor kings. But it was not until the Elizabethan era that, with the great general progress in administration, sanction was given for the conveyance of private mail and

15

parcels by royal messengers. The Queen's " Master of the Posts," Thomas Randolph, made sure, however, in an order issued in January 1583, that " no private letters must be conveyed or delivered before the Queen's packet is safely handed over," and he also warned his post riders " not to open, break up or ' embessil ' any private packet." The office of the Queen's Master of the Posts was one of profit. He charged very high rates for letters, paying very little to his postmasters and riders. London merchants, whose packets were often lost or stolen, embarked on running private mail services, which led to quarrels with the Master of the Posts.

It was not until 1635 that Charles I established a state monopoly for the post. Thomas Witherings was his first " Postmaster of England and Foreign Parts " and regular mail courses were established on the five main roads, from London to Edinburgh, Norwich, Bristol, Exeter and Holyhead. The charges were very reasonable, the rate for conveying a letter or parcel over a distance of under 80 miles was 2d., between 80 to 140 miles—4d., over 140 miles—6d., and " to the border of Scotland and beyond "—8d. A somewhat erratic postal communication was also established across the English Channel, mainly with France and Holland. The post ran weekly between London and the four provincial towns and twice weekly between London and Edinburgh. In spite of the low rates, Witherings made a fortune, although he was obliged to convey all the King's official mail free of charge.

In the 17th century the Post Office became such a profitable business that Oliver Cromwell leased it to John Manley for an annual rental of £10,000, and after the Restoration Charles II " farmed " it out to a Sussex man, Henry Bishop, for seven years at £21,000. In spite of the much increased rental, Bishop made a huge fortune, employed 47 clerks and a corps of riders. He is of great importance to philately because he introduced the first " postmark " (see illustration).

The next " farmer " of the Post Office was the Earl of Arlington, who paid the king £43,000 a year and yet did very well. Bishop's invention of the " postmark " was carried on by all his successors in various fashions. Until 1680, London had no local post; the General Letter Office (as the Post Office was then called) delivered the mail received to the addresses in London, but it had to be brought to the General Letter Office for dispatch and letters within the city had to be sent by servants or casual

EARLY BRITISH POSTMARKS

Top row, from left to right: A Bishop postmark; London Penny Post of William **Dockwra** (1680); General Post under Government Control (1794).

Bottom row, from left to right: Maltese Cross (the first cancellation in use from 1840 to 1844); Dated Town postmark of 1842; postmark after 1844 (the number refers to the town or post office.)

messengers. On April 1st, 1680, a London merchant, William Dockwra, established the private " London Penny Post," promising daily collection and delivery of local letters and parcels. He started his enterprise on April Fools' Day and, although many people believed that it would be doomed to failure, Dockwra made such an excellent job of the " London Post " that the Duke of York (later King James II), who had become Postmaster General, claimed that it was an infringement on the king's postal monopoly. He succeeded in suppressing it after a long litigation before the King's Bench of Justices. The " London Penny Post " became part of the General Post Office and subsequently the penny rate was doubled.

Dockwra had made an innovation of great importance—postmarks which not only included the date of the posting, but also the approximate time, for instance " Mor. 8 " (8 a.m.) or " Af. 4 " (4 p.m.) and he thus became the creator of the postmark as we know it today.

The great expansion of the postal services in Britain came in the 18th century with the introduction of mail-coaches in 1784. In the first half of the 19th century the Post Office took advantage of the vigorous progress in engineering and railway development and the first dispatch of mail by train was made in 1830 between Liverpool and Manchester, to be followed quickly on many other routes.

The postal rates, however, were very high, much higher than at the time of Withering's " Post Office of England and Foreign Parts." The charges were based on the distance a letter or parcel was carried. With the great expansion of commerce and industry during the early Victorian era, these high postal charges were a great disadvantage to trade and economic interests in the country and were strongly criticised by Parliament and the public.

It was Rowland Hill's great work of postal reform that

resulted not only in a cheap postal rate—calculated by weight and not by distance—but also in the creation of the first modern postal service in the world and, above all, in the introduction of the first postage stamp.

In 1840, a uniform inland rate of one penny per half-ounce came into operation and, to save the Post Office time and labour, Hill insisted that all mail must be pre-paid. Before that, payment was collected on delivery. To make the pre-payment easy and also to provide the Post Office with ready cash in advance, Hill decided that stamps should be affixed to letters and parcels as a form of receipt for the pre-payment

Thus the Penny Black was born. While it was being sold for the first time on May 6th, 1840, in London, the Post Office were issuing wrappers designed by William Mulready, a Royal artist. These were the first officially issued envelopes and letter-sheets combined, which did not require a postage stamp, because the payment for them included the postal rate.

The design of the " Mulready," showing Britannia sending out winged messengers to all parts of the world, surrounded by groups of colonial natives, elephants, camels, and women eagerly reading letters, proved un-popular and newspapers were full of scorn for the novelty. Yet the " Mulready " was a precursor of the postcard, letter-card and aerogram, which became extremely popular.

Three years passed before other countries began to follow the revolutionary introduction of the postage stamp by Britain. The enterprising Post Offices of the Swiss Cantons (before the establishment of the Federal Post Office) were the earliest followers. Zürich issued its first stamp on March 1st, 1843, Geneva on September 30th of the same year, Basle on July 1st, 1845. Strangely enough, it was Brazil that emulated Britain as the first large country, issuing the famous " Bull's-eye " stamps on July 1st, 1843, only a few months after Zürich.

In 1845 the Post Master of New York issued the first American local-post stamp; the first British colony to introduce postage stamps was Mauritius in 1847, followed by Bermuda in 1848. From 1849 many European countries followed suit, first Bavaria, Belgium and France, and a year later Austria, Hanover, Prussia, Saxony, Spain, as well as British Guiana and the first Australian State, Victoria.

During the next twenty years all civilised countries and many colonies used postage stamps and in 1874 the General Postal Union was founded, becoming a year later the Universal Postal Union. It is still the organisation linking all the post office authorities in the world, regulating the mail services between all countries, and serving as a clearing house for the financial arrangements between the postal authorities.

Rowland Hill, the great postal reformer became head of the British Post Office in 1854 and inaugurated many other services which have proved so beneficial to the British public, including the Post Office Savings Bank in 1861. He introduced the first letter boxes in London's main streets in 1855, laid the plans for the Money Order and Postal Order system and for the parcel service, which was introduced in 1885. By the end of the 19th century the regular delivery of mail was assured to every house in Britain.

Postal traffic increased enormously during the century after the introduction of the Penny Postage. Rowland Hill's rate remained unchanged until 1918, in spite of the substantial decline in the value of money over nearly 80 years.

In 1969 the Post Office handled over 11,000 million letters, in addition to about 200 million parcels and 45 million registered items. Every day it conveys and delivers about 35 million letters and each year it deals with an ever-increasing volume of Christmas mail. During the 1969 Christmas - New Year Season more than 900 million letters and cards were posted in a single week. Obviously, all the post office technical services had to be developed to match the needs of the traffic. In 1919 the G.P.O. established its own motor transport fleet for the collection and delivery of mail to and from sorting offices. This fleet numbered exactly 48 vans. By 1969 it had 20,000 motor vehicles.

The British Post Office, with its staff of some 400,000 is the oldest of Britain's state undertakings and its postal services are universally acclaimed as the best in the world. Its service to " foreign parts " now conveys more than 550 million items a year, fifty per cent of which travel by air.

The post offices of other great countries, such as the United States, France and Germany, are similarly rendering to mankind great international communication services and many smaller countries have excellent postal organisations of great importance to world traffic, for instance Switzerland, because a huge amount of mail goes in transit across the Alps, through the tunnels of St. Gotthard and Simplon which link Western and Northern Europe with the South and the South-East.

The progress of postal communications from the runners of Persian kings, Caesar's military couriers, the postal riders of the Middle Ages, from the mail coach and post train to jet aircraft, is part of man's history and civilisation.

CHAPTER 3

Different Kinds of Stamps

In the foregoing chapter we learned something about postal history and the advent of the " adhesive " Penny Black. This was the first postage stamp. But already in 1881 we find on the 1d. lilac the inscription " Postage and Inland Revenue," and postage stamps have been used in Britain, as well as in other countries, not only for the pre-payment of postal rates for the conveyance of mail but also for other purposes. In Britain, postage stamps can be used for the payment of certain Treasury duties, such as for receipts, bills of exchange, bank cheques, deeds and agreements.

While in Britain almost every kind of postal service can be pre-paid by using ordinary postage stamps (for instance when paying for a telegram), many foreign countries have issued special stamps for parcels, newspapers, express delivery fees, airmail rates and so on.

Most postal authorities, including the British G.P.O., have also issued special stamps for collecting additional payments for unfranked or insufficiently pre-paid mail, the so called " postage due stamps," and also stamps for the mail of government departments, which are called " official stamps."

Thus, apart from ordinary postage stamps the collector has to recognise many other categories. Moreover, among postage stamps valid for franking ordinary letter and parcel mail, the philatelist has to differentiate between " definitive " issues and stamps issued on special occasions, such as to commemorate a historical event, or in aid of a charitable fund.

The following short list gives a general classification of stamps used in connection with various postal services:

Airmail Stamps. With the great development of air transport most countries, including most of the British Commonwealth, issue special stamps for mail conveyed by air. These are dealt with in Chapter 10.

Postage Due Stamps. In Britain and most other countries special stamps are, or were, issued for collecting postage due. They are not sold to the public, unless at " philatelic counters " of the general post offices.

Official Stamps are used for franking mail of Government departments. They were introduced in Britain in 1882, but discontinued after 1904, and now British Government departments use envelopes marked " On Her Majesty's Service." Many other countries, however, use official stamps, usually current ordinary postage stamps overprinted with " Official " or " Service " in the language of the country.

Express Stamps. Some countries issue stamps for the payment of an additional fee for delivery by special messengers.

Newspaper Stamps. A number of countries issue stamps for the franking of newspapers and printed matter at reduced rates, but this custom is rapidly disappearing because of bulk posting and the growing use of meter marking and stamping machines.

Parcel Post Stamps are those issued for the franking of parcels and they are akin to " railway stamps."

Railway Stamps are issued by some foreign post offices, where agreements with State or private railway companies existed, or still exist, to convey parcels on behalf of the post office. In Britain, the Transport Commission uses its own labels.

Telegraph Stamps have been issued by some foreign countries for the pre-payment of telegrams.

While all these stamps serve different postal purposes, the philatelist recognises other groups within the category of postage stamps, although all these may be regarded by the post office as ordinary postage stamps. We can distinguish the following:

Commemorative Stamps are issued for normal postal purposes, but have, as a rule, a limited duration of their validity. There is no country in the world which has not issued stamps to commemorate either a historical anniversary, a political event, some important festival, conference, or international sport gathering.

Charity Stamps are issued by many countries at a price in excess of their face value. Thus, a charity stamp might have the face value of 20 centimes, but is sold by the post office at 25 centimes (the additional amount is often denoted in the design by " + 5c ", or the amount in question). This additional amount (or " surcharge ") is given by the Post Office to the charitable fund in aid of which the stamp is issued. Obviously, it is left to the generosity of the person who mails a letter whether to buy a charity stamp and thus make a donation, or to use an ordinary postage stamp.

Publicity Stamps. Some countries issue special stamps for the purpose of advertising either a State or private institution, or for publicising some governmental, social or educational enterprise. Some countries have issued " publicity stamps " for Road Safety campaigns, or to advertise a trade fair or an exhibition. During the last few years a number of European states have been issuing stamps of a similar design, to emphasise their economic co-operation (so called " Europa " stamps). The dividing line between " publicity stamps " and ordinary postage stamps depicting, for instance, beautiful scenery or industrial products (France has issued postage stamps with designs showing motives from her wine, perfume and jewellery industries; other countries " advertise " their tourist attractions) is obviously thin and many collectors will regard them as ordinary postage stamps.

Miniature Sheets. A number of foreign post offices issue, on special occasions, small sheets depicting one or two stamps, framed by ornamental designs and inscriptions. In most cases these sheets are gummed and can be used like stamps for franking the mail. But their face value is very much lower than their selling price, and the surplus is used either for charitable funds or for the financing of an exhibition or some such project. While collectors specialising in the stamps of a country will include " miniature sheets " in their albums, the general collector may disregard them.

*   *   *

The saying that " charity covers a multitude of sins " aptly applies to many charity stamps. Some countries, for instance New Zealand or Switzerland, have been issuing for many years a few charity stamps annually with a modest addition to the face value, in aid of anti-tuber-culosis campaigns, cancer research, educational funds, child care and so on. No one will grudge paying a penny or two in excess of the face value in cases like these.

But many countries issue " charity " sets in order to gain revenue from stamp collectors. Some of these sets, often comprising several high values, have been brought into disrepute either by the arbitrary limitation of the numbers printed, or the disproportionately high " charity " surcharge levied in addition to the face value. In several instances the postal authorities of certain countries sold the bulk of such issues to dealers who were then able to dictate the price to collectors and to create " rarities " which had no real right to this title. The same applies to certain " commemorative " stamps, which are issued exclusively for the doubtful benefit of stamp collectors.

While the British G.P.O. had, for almost a century, steadfastly refused to issue any but ordinary stamps, it yielded in 1924 to the then growing fashion of "commemoratives" by issuing two stamps for the British Empire Exhibition. Five years later, in 1929, five stamps, including a £1 value, appeared to commemorate the Postal Union Congress in London and other commemoratives followed on the occasion of the Silver Jubilee of King George V, the Coronation in 1936, the centenary of the Penny Postage, Victory celebration, the Olympic Games in 1948, the Royal Silver Wedding, and other events. On the occasion of the London International Stamp Exhibition in 1960, two attractive stamps commemorated the Tercentenary of the Post Office Charter, given in 1660 by King Charles II. More recently there have been special anniversary issues commemorating the erection of Westminster Abbey and the Battle of Hastings, both in 1066, and the Battle of Britain in 1940. The Investiture of the Prince of Wales on 1 July 1969 was marked by a special series. Other issues have featured British ships, landscapes, bridges, birds and wild flowers and there is also now a regular set of Christmas stamps. (See illustrations facing page 145).

Even though the issue of commemorative stamps by the British G.P.O. has increased in recent years, it still restricts itself to about six sets of special issues each year and its record is good in comparison with some countries whose stamp issues are produced solely for the collector's album.

Countries such as Monaco and some South American republics commemorate events which have nothing to do with their own history. Why, for instance, should the Monaco Post Office celebrate the 80th birthday of Dr. Albert Schweitzer with a set of four stamps, including a top value of 200 francs? Or why did Nicaragua issue a set of six stamps and an airmail set of five " in homage to President Roosevelt." depicting him as a stamp collector, browsing through his album? The answer is, of course, that a very large proportion of commemorative and charity stamps are printed for sale to collectors and that the post offices of some countries reap a golden harvest without rendering any postal service, because most of these stamps are collected in " mint " condition, or cancelled " to order," and never used for franking a letter.

In 1961 a number of philatelic associations in Britain and abroad decided to refuse to regard some of these issues as authentic, and several catalogue publishers have refused to include purely speculative issues in their lists.

Amongst the worst culprits in releasing an unending flow of so called commemoratives are some of the States of the Persian Gulf, a number of Latin American countries, and several of the Communist countries. It must be left to the judgment of the individual collector whether he accepts or rejects such colourful but frequently valueless speculative issues.

An important category of stamps are those overprinted or surcharged. In most cases they are ordinary stamps used for postal purposes, but issued, or re-issued, with an overprint for some particular reason.

For instance, there may be a change in the currency. During the inflation period in Poland and Germany in 1923 many stamps of low face value were overprinted with a surcharge denoting the new inflated value. Thus we find Polish stamps of 2 Marks, 5 Marks, 10 Marks and 20 Marks surcharged with " 20,000 Mk.", " 50,000 Mk." and " 100,000 Mk." Germany issued a long series of such surcharges reaching the astronomic figures of 500,000,000 Marks and even 1, 2, 5, 20 and 50 Milliard Marks. In 1912 Portugal changed her currency from " Reis " to " Centavos " and " Escudos " and a number of surcharged stamps were issued denoting the new values. Similarly, a currency change occurred in Lithuania in 1922, from " Skatiku " and " Auksinas " to " Cents " and " Litas," and fifty stamps were overprinted. A more recent example is the change of the Pound Sterling currency to a decimal system currency in South Africa which led to the hurried overprints of the stamps of Basutoland, Bechuanaland and Swaziland.

But a much more frequent reason for surcharging existing values is a change in the postal rates. Before destroying many millions of stamps, the postal authority might decide to use the obsolete value by re-issuing them with an overprint denoting the new face value. This happens in almost every country, and because of their temporary character— and because in due course they are replaced by new " definitive " stamps of the required face values—such stamps are sometimes referred to as " Provisionals."

Overprints may also be used because of a change in the constitution of a country. For example, after a revolution a stamp showing the portrait of a monarch would be overprinted with the word " Republic." Similarly, during wars, stamps of an invaded or occupied country may be overprinted by the enemy.

In some cases ordinary postage stamps are overprinted with an inscription referring to an anniversary, exhibition or other event, or surcharged with an additional payment in aid of some fund. Such an overprint or surcharge would turn them into either commemorative or charity stamps. Another example among British stamps is the " England Winners " overprint on the 4d. stamp of the 1966 World Cup Football Competition issue.

There are many other " special " stamps which would deserve classification but they concern the more advanced philatelist. Among them are Military Post Stamps, Soldiers stamps (issued by some countries to servicemen to allow the sending of mail free of charge); registration stamps, stamps issued for statistical purposes and for the training of postal employees, special stamps for the use of Members of Parliament (issued at one time in Spain), and " franco " labels issued to hospital patients or prisoners of war.

Finally, there are " bogus stamps," issued by private persons or committees who claim the right to represent a postal authority, although they do not exercise any postal service. For instance, a " Revolutionary Committee " in New York (in partnership with a stamp dealer) issued several attractive sets for a non-existent " Republic of Molucca," in anticipation of the conquest of that territory from the Republic of Indonesia. Likewise a Committee of anti-Titoist Croats in the United States, printed stamps of a " Free Croatia," one of the federated states of Yugoslavia.

However, not all stamps issued by a private organisation or even a commercial company are bogus stamps. Owners of small islands without a post office, hotel managers in the Swiss Alps, seaport authorities and so on, have issued "local stamps" for the payment of a fee for the dispatch of letters and parcels by messengers to the mainland or the nearest post office. These " local stamps " or " semi-postals " are used for genuine postal services and are collected by specialists.

As we shall see in Chapter 6, there is a lengthy and complex technical process before a stamp arrives at a post office counter. After the artist has completed his design, printing plates are prepared from which proofs are made. Sometimes a number of designs are selected and only one approved after several " essays " have been produced. Specialists include in their albums such " essays " and " proofs." Neither are ever sold to the public by the postal authorities but, somehow or other, they do occasionally find their way into the hands of philatelists and, in many cases, are very rare.

Reprints of old and sometimes rare stamps are made from original plates, blocks or stones of an issue after these stamps have been withdrawn from circulation, often a long time ago. Some postal authorities destroy the original plates or stones, others retain them and allow specimens to be reprinted for sale to collectors. Although they are made from the original plates or stones, they can usually be distinguished from the original issues because they are printed on " modern " paper and with " modern " inks.

Needless to say a reprint—while meriting collecting as a curiosity—is not the genuine article and can be bought sometimes for a few pence, while the originally issued stamp, made from the same block or stone, may be a rarity worth many hundreds of pounds. There are, however, reprints which are valuable because of the very small quantity produced.

Even experts sometimes have difficulty in recognising reprints of stamps from some of the early German Sates, because these reprints were made fairly soon after the stamps had been withdrawn and their paper, ink and printing method were very similar to those used at the first printing.

The beginner and less experienced collector will be well advised not to be tempted by the very low price of a classic rarity in good condition. With the growing number of collectors, classic stamps are in increasingly short supply and their prices mount every year by leaps and bounds. Hence a " cheap " classic stamp will either be a reprint or a forgery, and before acquiring such a doubtful " rarity " the collector should submit it for examination to the expert committees of either the Royal Philatelic Society or the British Philatelic Association.

CHAPTER 4

The Collector's Tools

Many stamps which today would make the collector's heart miss a beat and would represent a small fortune, have been destroyed for ever in the grubby schoolboys' hands of our grandfathers.

Seventy or eighty years ago, even after half a century had passed since the first postage stamp was issued and stamp collecting had reached a fairly advanced stage, stamps were still treated very roughly. They were stuck into an album with a lump of flour paste, with their corners broken, having been taken out of a pocket or tobacco pouch, folded or crumpled.

The condition of a stamp is of the utmost importance. A broken or torn stamp—even if the tear is quite small—or one which is " thinned " (i.e. the paper having a thin spot), is either worthless or, in the case of a rarity, of very much less value.

A collector must, therefore, observe the first law of philately: never to touch a stamp with the fingers but to handle it by using tweezers. Handling stamps with the fingers will damage the fine " teeth " of the perforated edges. Mint stamps are easily spoiled by a touch of the fingers, because our skin is often slightly moist. Some stamps are printed on chalk-surfaced paper and, again, handling almost inevitably results in damaging the delicate surface.

After a little practice the beginner will find that handling stamps with tweezers is an easy and convenient method. A pair of good, stainless steel or chromium-plated tweezers can be bought for as little as 2/- at any stamp shop. Do not buy tweezers at a chemist's shop, because those with sharply pointed or thick, corrugated ends, designed for medical purposes or the removal of hair, are quite unsuitable.

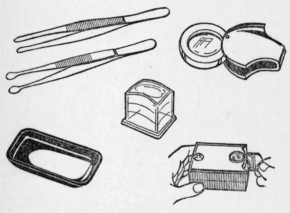

COLLECTOR'S TOOLS

Two types of tweezers, two kinds of magnifying glass, a black tray, and an electric watermark detector into which the stamp is inserted on a slide and illuminated from below by a battery-powered lamp.

Another collector's tool, which a beginner may already possess, is a magnifying glass. This will help him to recognise the details of the design and it is essential to the advanced collector for ascertaining flaws, varieties, errors and, of course, the condition of a stamp. Magnifying glasses are sold in a wide range of prices, from plastic ones for a few pence to achromatic precision lenses which

SOME FIRST ISSUES

Top row: The Penny Black, the first adhesive stamp, issued in 1840; the first United States 10 cents of 1847; the first 10 c. of France, 1849. *Second Row:* one of the first stamps of Ceylon, 4 pence, of 1857; the 1 kreuzer of Bavaria, of 1849; one of the first Swiss Cantonal stamps, the 6 rappen of Zurich, 1843. *Bottom Row:* One of the earliest Italian States stamps, the 5 c. of Sardinia, 1851; the first stamp issued in Canada by the province of New Brunswick in 1851; the famous 1d. orange-red of Mauritius, 1847.

COMMEMORATIVE STAMPS

Top: a Greek stamp commemorating the centenary of Lord Byron's death; one of five special stamps issued on the occasion of the investiture of Prince Charles as Prince of Wales. *Second row:* a Mexican stamp commemorating the 1968 Olympic Games in Mexico; a British stamp commemorating the opening of the Post Office Tower in 1965. *Left:* a stamp from Luxemburg issued for the 1936 congress of the International Philatelic Federation.

might be quite expensive. A very useful one is connected to a handle containing a small torch so that the stamp placed under the lens is lit up.

To measure perforations the collector uses special gauges. The first one was invented by the great French philatelist, Professor Legrand, and has since been much improved. The value of a stamp might depend on the perforation, because it often happens that sheets are perforated by several machines; the reasons for this are described in Chapter 6.

The use of a perforation gauge, which can be bought for a shilling, can be mastered after a few minutes practice. The gauge is a small card on which rows of black dots are printed, corresponding to the most frequent perforations found on stamps. By placing a stamp face down on one of the rows of dots and moving it upwards or downwards until the dots fit exactly with the " holes " of the perforation, its number is ascertained. Most stamps have 10 to 14 perforation holes, but there are also fractional perforations between these numbers, and the standard gauge gives scales from 8 to 16½, including quarter perforations between each number (see illustration p.34).

Some stamps have the same perforation at the top and bottom but a different one at the left and right sides. We speak then of a stamp being perforated, for instance, 13½ by 14, the first figure always referring to the top and bottom, the second to the side perforation.

Finding and recognising a watermark sometimes presents a more difficult problem. Many stamps have only a very faint watermark, hardly visible to the naked eye, particularly in the case of used stamps which are heavily cancelled. A magnifying glass will help to show it up, but more often the stamp will have to be placed on a watermark detector. Specially manufactured detectors can be bought (see illustration p.32) but a smooth black piece of metal or a clean black tile will do just as well. The stamp is placed face downwards, moistened with water and the watermark will then show up darker than the rest of the paper. If it still appears only faintly, the stamp should be carefully

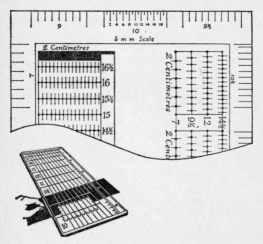

PERFORATION GAUGE

Above is the upper half of a typical gauge. The dots on the gauge must correspond with the punched-out holes of the stamp perforation. Below is a more recent gauge in use. The lines of the gauge must correspond with the centre of the perforation holes.

dried between two sheets of blotting paper, replaced on the black "detector" and then a few drops of benzine or carbon tetrachloride poured on its reverse side. However, chemicals must not be used in the case of chalk paper or on stamps printed with certain dyes, because the paper can be damaged or the ink made to run.

There are many more complex tools used by experts to ascertain varieties, forgeries, or the "doctoring" of rarities. The Quartz lamp, the microscope, the micrometer, electronic apparatus, photomicrography and X-rays are used in scientific examination of stamps to distinguish minute differences in the texture of the paper, inking, printing, etc., and above all in detecting forgeries and faked overprints and postmarks.

A colour guide is another collector's tool. It helps to find out the different shades, in accordance with those listed in catalogues. A useful one containing seventy-five standard colours is available for a few shillings.

A few small trays (made of plastic material and available in multiple stores at a small outlay) will be found handy for sorting stamps. But the shallow lids of cardboard boxes measuring about 4 ins. by 8 ins. will do quite well instead. Stamps should not be scattered about on a table because, quite apart from the danger that they might be soiled, a sudden draught from an open door or window might scatter them far and wide.

Stamps must not be kept without proper protection in wallets, notebooks or between the pages of a pocket diary. Even experienced philatelists do this sometimes, but it is a bad habit. Newly acquired stamps, whether mint or used, should be put immediately into a little transparent envelope. These envelopes are sold in many sizes and cost little. They provide excellent protection and are of particular use for the initial sorting by country, issue, shade, and so on.

One can easily build a temporary store for loose stamps by using a box of an appropriate size and stacking the envelopes in the way index cards are stored. Cards, slightly larger than the envelopes, protruding half an inch, can be used to separate batches of the transparent envelopes. The name of the country, date of issue, etc. can be written on the card. Never write on the transparent envelope itself, certainly not using a ball-point pen or a sharpened pencil, as the writing could be impressed upon the stamp inside and might ruin it.

With his tools at hand, his stamps in trays and transparent envelopes on his working table, the collector can now proceed to find more permanent accommodation for his stamps. If he wants to store them temporarily, but in proper order according to their catalogue numbers and, perhaps also their shades and varieties, he will put them into a stock book.

There is a great variety of stock books available at stamp shops, from quite small ones—which can be carried in the breast-pocket—to large books of album size with many pages. The stock-book pages are made of stiff cardboard with linen or transparent paper strips, into which the stamps are slipped. The pages are either fast bound to the cover or they are loose, put between a spring back cover. If the strips are on both sides of a page, transparent interleaves should be used to protect the stamps on the left page from getting rubbed or entangled with those on the right page.

Mint or unused stamps with part-gum must, of course, not be soaked, but most used stamps—though there are some exceptions—should get a clean bath in cold water before they are stored or mounted. This applies only to stamps which have either already been removed from the envelope or wrapper or to those which the collector has cut from an envelope.

In many cases, the " entire " (i.e. the whole wrapper or envelope) will be preserved in its original state, e.g. if the envelope is a First Day Cover, a flown cover, bears a special postmark or has a particularly interesting and attractive combination of stamps. There are many collectors who specialise in collecting "entires", and in the case of rare stamps their value on an "entire" is often many times that of a loose stamp.

Never peel a stamp from the envelope or adhering paper with your fingernails or tweezers. A stamp man-handled in such a manner will inevitably be damaged. If the stamp is cut out, a small paper margin on all four sides should be left. Then the piece is put into the bath—a plastic tray or any suitable piece of crockery such as a soup plate or a shallow pudding basin will do. After a few minutes the stamp will part from the paper without any assistance. If it does not, after a good soaking, you may remove it gently by sliding it off the paper, provided that no force has to be applied. Otherwise leave it for another few minutes in the water and try again.

The wet stamp or stamps should now be lifted with the tweezers and placed between pages of a good quality, fairly thick, white blotting paper. But before doing this, you should make sure that no trace of gum is still adhering to the back, otherwise the stamp will stick to the blotting paper and the soaking procedure will have to be repeated. Never use coloured blotting paper for drying, because it could happen that a faint hue of the colour might be transferred to the stamp and it would become a useless freak.

Only when the stamp is completely dry, should it be removed to the stock book, envelope or album. The album will, in the end, provide its permanent home and in the following chapter this is dealt with in greater detail. The stamps will be mounted on the pages of an album,— whether it be a modest exercise book or a luxurious, expensively leather-bound volume—only by means of specially-made gummed hinges.

As I mentioned, in the early days of philately stamps

were stuck into albums with glue, flour-paste or crude gum. Many old stamps and rarities were thus ruined. It happened on occasions that someone found, in an old trunk in the attic, a small album full of rare stamps dating sixty or eighty years before. Perhaps it was just grand-dad's schoolboy collection. It might have been a real treasure-trove today but for the lamentable condition of the stamps fastened with a blob of black glue or with paste that had become as hard as a piece of cement.

Now the use of hinges is a universal law among philatelists. The hinges are made of pellucid paper, gummed on one side. There are many qualities and several sizes and it is advisable to spend a few pence more and to buy the best quality. A good hinge will have the finest gum that will not affect the stamp's paper, or, in the case of a mint stamp, its own gum. Hinges are sold either flat or ready folded. Many collectors prefer to fold them themselves and attach to a mint stamp only a very small portion of the hinge. The gum of a hinge is pure and tasteless and made in such a way that the high-quality hinge will peal off easily from the stamp and the album page, if and when it becomes necessary to remove the stamp.

A little skill must be applied in attaching the hinge correctly. Lay the stamp face downwards. Fold the hinge about one third of its size across. With your lip—not with the tip of your tongue—very slightly moisten the shorter (one third) part of the hinge and press it on to the upper part of the stamp, a fraction of an inch below the top. Then lift the stamp with your tweezers, moisten the last third of the longer part of the hinge and press it gently to the space where you want to have the stamp mounted. As part of the hinge will have remained dry and is not sticking either to the stamp or to the paper, the stamp can be lifted up on its hinge with the tweezers. It should be left in this position for a few minutes until both moistened parts of the hinge are completely dry. This will prevent any excess of moisture oozing out. It is of particular importance when mounting mint stamps, because otherwise the

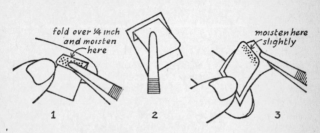

MOUNTING

Lay stamp face downwards. 1. Fold hinge about a $\frac{1}{3}$ of its way across and moisten this folded part slightly. 2. Press on to stamp a fraction of an inch below the top. 3. Moisten lower $\frac{1}{3}$ of hinge. Press gently on to space where you wish stamp to be mounted.

surfeit of moisture coming from beneath the hinge could make the stamp stick fast to the paper by its own gum. The condition of the mint stamp would thus be ruined.

There are other methods of attaching the hinge. Using the unfolded hinge, moisten one third or less of it and stick it to the top of the stamp. Then, with the hinge still unfolded, and holding stamp and adhering hinge with the tweezers, moisten a short strip of the hinge at its other end. With the hinge pointing down and the stamp still face down, press the moistened part of the hinge to the album page. Only then fold the hinge with a turn of the tweezers, thus reversing the stamp from back to front, again waiting a few moments until the gum of the hinge has dried. This method is preferable with perforated stamps, because it prevents any of the top " teeth " of the stamp being folded with the hinge.

To " wet-mouth " collectors I must give the warning to be particularly careful when mounting mint stamps. Even a small excess of moisture can be disastrous. Practice makes perfect, and a properly mounted collection enhances not only its appearance but also its value. If the collector decides to dispose of part of his collection, either by offering it to a dealer, in an auction, or to another collector, he must expect that every serious philatelist will carefully examine the way in which the stamps have been mounted.

In the foregoing chapter I discussed the main categories of stamps, but " sorting " is much more than merely separating them by countries and into the main groups, such as ordinary postage stamps, airmail stamps, commemoratives and so on. Obviously, if mounting in an album which does not provide framed spaces and illustrations for the many issues, the collector will want to find the date of issue, the sequence of a stamp in a set and, very soon also, the main varieties of the same stamp.

For this we need a catalogue. It is much more than a collector's tool. It is his trusted and constant companion and adviser. With the multitude of issues which have appeared over more than a century, collecting stamps without a catalogue is today quite impractical.

A stamp catalogue is basically a stamp dealer's price list. But, in fact, it has developed into a philatelic handbook and there are today many highly specialised catalogues, listing not only every stamp but many of the varieties, flaws and errors of designs, differences in watermarks, perforation and colour.

In the English-speaking world the two most complete and reliable catalogues are published by Stanley Gibbons Ltd., of London, and Scott Co., Inc., of New York. The

Stanley Gibbons " Simplified " Whole World catalogue is published every year in the autumn, while several other editions, containing more detailed lists and including a number of the most important varieties, are published in separate volumes, one containing the stamp issues of Great Britain and the British Commonwealth, another of Europe and the colonies of European states, a third of America and the independent countries of Asia and Africa, and a fourth dealing exclusively with stamps of the reign of Elizabeth II, is called the *Elizabethan*. For collectors of British stamps Stanley Gibbons have also now produced a handy and inexpensive " Check List " based on the main catalogue.

There are several excellent general catalogues in foreign languages, such as the Yvert & Tellier Catalogue (French), the Michel Catalogue (German) and the Zumstein Europe Catalogue (German). There are a host of catalogues devoted to single countries or groups of countries, the British Commonwealth, France, Switzerland, United States, etc., and many handbooks, some dealing with only one issue or even one single stamp.

For the beginner even a slightly out of date catalogue—perhaps a gift from another collector who has acquired the latest edition for himself—may give good service for a while. It will, of course, not give him the most recent valuations, as prices of stamps change from year to year, neither will it contain new issues of the last few years. It will, however, be a guide to all stamps which appeared prior to the date of its publication. Stamp catalogues are not expensive and the outlay of about £2 for a new one will be amply rewarded. For the beginner a " Simplified Gibbons " will suffice, until he decides to turn his interest to a group of countries or embark upon specialising in one country. Then he will require catalogues which contain more detailed lists.

The catalogue lists the dates of every issue, illustrates one or several stamps of each issue, gives descriptions of the designs and, as a rule, the purpose or reason for the issue. The face value of each stamp is given, then follows the colour (in more detailed catalogues, some of the most important varieties and shades are mentioned) and, finally, in two columns the " quotation," e.g. the estimated market value. The first column gives the price for the mint, the second for the stamp used in the post.

Each stamp has a catalogue number. This is very convenient, because a collector who wants to buy a stamp from a dealer or exchange stamps with another amateur needs only to mention the catalogue and the number to identify the stamp. Thus " G.B. S.G. (Simpl.) No. 205 " means that it is a stamp issued by Great Britain and listed in the Stanley Gibbons Simplified Catalogue under No. 205. In this instance, it is the 4 pence green and brown, issued in 1887 with a portrait of Queen Victoria. Similarly, " Brazil S.G. 749 " is sufficient to describe a stamp issued by the Brazilian Post Office on March 19th, 1943, to commemorate the 400th anniversary of the discovery of the River Amazon, at a face value of 40 centavos, showing the map of the tributaries of the river, designed by R. Pinheiro, printed by the typographic process, in orange-brown colour, on paper bearing the watermark " Brasil Correio " and stars, and perforated 11. All these details are given in the Stanley Gibbons Catalogue, Part III, listed under No. 749.

While no collector should become a slave of the catalogue, most of us have arranged our collections according to catalogue numbers, and the beginner will be well advised to follow suit. As he advances in the pursuit of the hobby and becomes a specialist, he will discover that there are many varieties, shades and minor flaws which even the most detailed catalogues do not include. He will then have in his collection " uncatalogued " stamps, the value of which might be difficult to determine. But this will be an exception and not the rule, and the catalogue will remain his almost exclusive guide, until he takes to the study of philatelic literature and finds in special handbooks some reference to the " uncatalogued " stamp.

Catalogue reading needs a little practice. The beginner may quickly decide that he has an " uncatalogued " stamp, and believe that he has found a great rarity among his humble specimens. He will soon discover that he has looked in the catalogue under a wrong heading and that his " find " is duly catalogued and valued at fourpence or less. Sometimes a stamp design is only slightly altered in a later issue and the catalogue then only refers to " similar design as No. 153, but with frame rounded in the corners " or " with letters without serifs," or some such thing. The only way of avoiding mistakes by assuming that the stamp in question is a strange " variety " rather than one with a slightly altered but catalogued design, is to read the catalogue as often as possible and acquaint oneself with the methods of its listing and lay-out. Quite a few advanced philatelists go to bed every night with their " S.G." and study it year after year, like the Holy Bible. Indeed, the catalogue is the collector's gospel.

The catalogue " quotations," or prices, are not necessarily the market values of stamps. They are the valuation of a stamp in perfect condition and, if used, with a very fine postmark. In the case of old issues, neither the condition nor the cancellation will, as a rule, be perfect. The real value of a rarity quoted in a catalogue at, say, £100, might be only £2, simply because the condition of the stamp is poor. Even modern stamps are often offered much below catalogue value, for a similar reason. In exchange deals, when no money changes hands, a collector will have to agree with his friend the value of the stamps to be exchanged, using the catalogue quotation as a basis, but taking into account the condition of his own specimens and those offered to him by his friend in exchange.

Catalogue quotations do not, of course, take into consideration "tired" stamps or stamps which have, in any way, been "doctored." As old stamps are getting more and more rare and difficult to come by, quite apart from the fact that in pristine condition their price might be beyond the pocket of an ordinary collector, one is sometimes tempted to acquire a "tired" stamp, for instance an imperforate whose paper is rubbed or thinned, which has bland corners, or is "close cut," that is, whose margins are very small or missing altogether.

Many rare stamps have been "doctored." This amounts to making a thinned or torn stamp look as near perfect as possible and has been done sometimes extremely skilfully. If the tear is small, it can be made almost invisible. A crumpled stamp can be pressed or ironed, a thinned one cured by spreading paper pulp on the thin spot and so on.

Although a collector may decide to include a "tired" or "doctored" stamp in his album because he realises that he will never be able to acquire a perfect or near-perfect specimen to fill that exasperating gap on the album page, he must realise that his acquisition is either worthless, or in the case of great rarities, worth only a fraction of the catalogue value.

In exceptional circumstances catalogue values can work the other way too. Sometimes it is quite impossible to buy a particular stamp at the catalogue price and in order to purchase a copy one must offer considerably more than the catalogue price. It has been known for a stamp-dealer to offer more than three times the catalogue price in order to obtain a modern but obsolete British Colonial stamp.

CHAPTER 5

A Good Home for your Stamps

With his first accumulation of stamps sorted by countries
and (if only roughly) according to issues and catalogue
numbers in transparent envelopes or in a stock book, the
beginner will now decide to find a more permanent home
for his treasures.

Many famous collectors started with nothing else but a
schoolboy's exercise book. It is, in many ways, preferable
to use a few exercise books—either with unlined or
faintly checked pages—than to buy one of the cheapest
printed " junior albums." These albums provide only one
page for a country, sometimes even lumping together two
or three British colonies or smaller foreign countries on a
single page.

The printed page headings are quite attractive and
include illustrations of stamps, but the beginner will soon
discover that this home for his stamps is extremely
cramped. After a while, when he has acquired a number
of common stamps of a large country, say France
or Germany, he will have no space to mount them.
But if he has several exercise books—one for Great
Britain, one for the Commonwealth, one for Western
Europe, and so on, these modest homes will be much
more roomy.

There are many " juvenile " albums, which are well
planned, contain several pages for every important
country and a number of stamp pictures. While not exactly
expensive, they cost more than the cheap soft-bound
" junior " albums sold in multiple stores. All printed

albums published in Britain cater for the general collector and contain all countries—with the exception of large Great Britain and British Commonwealth albums, which are published in several volumes and cost about £2 each.

The beginner, buying a printed album, will have to decide whether he wants to be a general collector, collecting all stamps issued anywhere in the world, or whether he wants, from the start to limit his scope.

In the first chapter we discussed the problem of " what shall we collect." If at the start the decision is made to limit the scope to either a group of countries, for instance the British Commonwealth, or a continent, for instance Europe or South America, then the only way to house such a collection is in an album with blank pages, or to buy one or more printed albums published abroad. British album publishers provide special albums for Britain and the Commonwealth only, but several German, French, Dutch and Swiss firms publish " single country albums," e.g. for the stamps of only France and her colonies, or Germany, or Denmark and so on. The headings are sometimes in several languages, including English.

But, in preference to any printed album, I recommend albums which contain blank pages. Even the best printed album provides spaces only for " normal " stamps. The collector who desires to practice philately more seriously and to include a few varieties, shades, or examples of different watermarks or perforation, will find that a printed album does not allow him sufficient space.

There are many unprinted albums ranging from inexpensive ones to de luxe editions bound in leather and containing stiff card pages, costing as much as £15 each. The selection of an album will depend on the pocket of the collector. Excellently produced albums can be bought for about 30/-, consisting of a well-made cover and between 60 and 100 pages of good quality blank leaves.

Nearly all these albums are loose-leaf albums. The pages can be removed and replaced easily. This is important, because if the beginner has provided only two or three pages for a country and if his collection of that country grows, he can simply insert several more pages. If this happens with other countries, he can then take out two or three countries and put these pages, with a few additional blank ones, into a new cover. Covers and pages are sold separately.

Loose-leaf albums are made in two binding systems, either with spring-backs or with a peg system, the latter similar to office box-files. It is a matter of personal preference which system to choose. The spring-back album has the advantage that the pages can be removed and replaced very quickly. On the other hand, if the spring becomes less springy with wear and tear, the pages are not held so securely together as in a peg-fitting cover. Loose-leaf pages, which can be bought separately, are supplied in many qualities and price ranges depending on whether they are fluted or hinged. The collector will be well advised to spend a little more on good quality and choose hinged pages. They are fastened to a linen hinge which ensures that each page lies flat when the album is opened. Some collectors like black paper or cartridge leaves, so-called " jet leaves." Nearly all album leaves are ruled with a faint criss-cross of lines, 1/32 inch apart, called " quadrillé." This is extremely helpful, both for placing the stamps symmetrically and for writing-up.

The arrangement of stamps on a page is very important. In a printed album, mounting is determined by rigid frames. On a blank page the collector can place the stamps according to his own taste. But there are certain rules which, if followed even only broadly, will greatly help the less experienced collector to achieve a pleasant presentation. Some people just mount one stamp after another, separating them perhaps only by sets. This makes for a crowded and dull presentation.

The first rule is: Do not overload a page with stamps. Not more than six stamps should be mounted in a row. Each issue, mounted chronologically, should be separated from the next one. If, therefore, an issue consists of a set of seven stamps, and the next issue of nine stamps, the lay-out could be thus:

```
1   2   3   4   5   6
7
1   2   3   4   5   6
7   8   9
```

But, although not overcrowded, the page would look unattractive because of its asymmetrical arrangement. Hence, philatelists have devised " formations " in which stamps can be arranged which are much more pleasing to the eye. There are various formations and a collector will find out for himself which formation suits his taste and at the same time enables him to accommodate the stamps of one or several issues on a single page. Often, there is one single stamp issued on the occasion of an anniversary, or because of a change in colour of an already existing similar design. It will be necessary to find a space for it within a formation.

Taking the two sets, one of seven and the other of nine stamps, a pleasing formation would be thus:

VARIOUS KINDS OF STAMPS

Apart from postage stamps for ordinary mail, many countries issue stamps for special purposes, such as for franking government mail, newspapers and printed matter, postage dues for insufficient pre-payment, and for express delivery. The illustrations show some of these "special" stamps which are described in Chapter 3. Sometimes stamps are overprinted or surcharged, like the two in the bottom row, because of a change in the constitution of a country, or in the postal rates.

SOME PUZZLES TO SOLVE

Some stamps provide few clues to their origin. Some are "dumb," like the top two illustrated, the "Bull's eye" of Brazil, 1843, and a newspaper stamp issued by Austria. Russian, Bulgarian and Greek stamps have inscriptions in cyrillic characters and many stamps of Arab and Far Eastern countries are not easy to recognise, such as those illustrated (*in the bottom row*) of Iran, Hyderabad and Japan.

```
          1   2   3

        4   5   6   7

    1   2   3   4   5

        6   7   8

            9
```

The last stamp (No. 9) will probably be a " high value,"
for instance, in a British Colonial issue, a £1 or 10/-
stamp. Placing it separately will show off this " high
value " nicely.

Or let's assume a really long set has to be mounted on a
page, without breaking it up. The formation may then be
thus:

```
            1   2   3

      4   5   6   7   8   9   10

        11  12  13  14  15

          16  17  18  19

      20  21  22  23  24  25

        26  27  28  29
```

If a single stamp or an issue of two is to be combined
on the same page with a set of several values, a number of
combinations is possible and, at times, the collector might
decide to alter slightly the chronological sequence. For
instance, if the first set of 4 stamps was issued in 1953, a
large single stamp in 1957 and the other set of 7 stamps in
1956, the formation might be thus:

1 2 3 4

1

1 2 3

4 5 6 7

The single stamp can be mounted in the centre of the page, giving pride of place, even if it ought, according to the date of issue, to follow the second set.

Often a set may consist of stamps of different sizes or shapes. Here the arrangement might be a little more difficult and it might even be necessary to alter the proper sequence of values, so that a large stamp of a lower value might be placed between two smaller or differently shaped stamps of higher face value.

There is, indeed, an infinite variety in the formations and the only rigid rule is to avoid overcrowding and to space the stamps attractively. There should always be at least one quarter of an inch between each stamp and about half-an-inch between the rows. Do not mount more than six rows on an album page of 10¾ by 9¼ in. (which is the standard size of most smaller albums) or seven rows on a page 11⅛ by 9¼ in. (which is another very common size).

The number of rows and the distance between them will, of course, depend on the " writing up," because there may sometimes be two or even three lines of text, describing an issue. This may take nearly as much space as a row of stamps. Again, some space should be left between the text and the stamp row above and below it.

The disadvantage of a blank leaves album is that just to mount stamps on the blank pages, without even the name of the country or date of issue, would not make a pleasing collection. It will be necessary to " write-up "

STAMP LAYOUTS

Four examples of how various sizes and shapes of stamps in different sets can be laid out attractively on the page.

the collection. Either every page or the first page of each country will bear as a heading the name of the country, perhaps with a line or two added, such as " Kingdom " or " Republic," geographical position, population, capital, currency, etc.

Writing-up is one of the great pleasures of philately, because it gives the collector an opportunity to put down on record what he has learned about his stamps. Moreover, if he wants to show his collection, either to another amateur, at a club display, or to a friend who knows little or nothing about stamps, pages full of stamps without a line of description would be almost meaningless.

Certain rules must be observed about writing-up. Verbosity and overloading the spaces between the stamp rows with text must be avoided. An album is a collection of stamps and not a handbook on philately. One or two explanatory lines above the first row of an issue will be quite sufficient, for instance, for a set of commemoratives issued by Australia:

1936 (August 3rd) Centenary of South Australia.
Recess printed, Wmk. CA, Perf. 11½

The second line refers to the method of printing, mentions the watermark and perforation, but can be left out if the collector decides not to go for the " technicalities." He might, instead, prefer to put beneath each of the three stamps of this issue a brief description of their designs, as follows:

ADELAIDE   *OLD GUM TREE*   *ADELAIDE*
in 1836   *Glenelg*   *King William St.*

However, writing-up the designs of each stamp in a long set might be a cumbersome business and sometimes repetitive, because many sets have several stamps of a similar design, showing the portrait of a king or president in different poses.

Even in the heading there may be some variations. For instance in the case of Canada, the first page for the stamps issued between 1851 and 1864 will be headed " Canada, British Colony in North America," while subsequent pages will be headed " The Dominion of Canada," because in 1867 the provinces of Canada were united with New Brunswick and Nova Scotia (which until then issued their own stamps).

When writing-up the pages the collector should work closely on the lines of the catalogue and use accepted " philatelic terms." A glossary of terms has been published by the Philatelic Congress of Great Britain (Blandford Press, London). Apart from using it for writing-up, it will be found very helpful.

Writing-up can be done either before or after mounting the stamps. It is better to do it before the stamps are fixed, because of the danger of soiling a stamp by an ink blot. Mounting and writing-up should always be a combined operation as regards the arrangement.

Finally, a word about the various methods of writing-up. Not every collector is a lettering artist. If he can write nicely, either in block letters, copperplate or the now fashionable italic, then he will do the writing-up by hand, using Indian ink and a fine mapping pen.

A ball-pen can be used, but most of the cheaper ball-point pens write rather thickly and, because of the pressure which has to be applied, cause pressure lines at the back of the album page. When using ball-pens each page should be taken out and the writing should be done on a hard surface, preferably a zinc plate or a piece of hardboard.

If the collector does not trust his own hand, he might use a stencil outfit, which is sold in drawing office shops and by many stamp dealers. There are also gummed labels on sale, printed with the titles of countries and, in the last resort, the album pages can be written up by typewriter.

According to his taste the collector can adorn the album with many minor additions. If he is a good draughtsman, he might draw on the first page of a country collection a

BRITISH NEW GUINEA

British New Guinea

British New Guinea

British New Guinea

ALBUM LETTERING

The top example is a printed gummed label which can be bought in any stamp shop and attached to the page. The other three are examples of different varieties of hand lettering which can be successfully executed after a little practice.

map of it, add the national flag, etc. One or two philatelic publishers provide maps and flags of most countries printed on gummed paper, and they can be cut out and stuck on the page.

Some collectors do not mount the stamps directly on the album page but on small pieces of black paper, cut to a size slightly larger than the stamp, and then mount these black "frames" on the album page. Again, people with a steady hand can attempt to frame every stamp. But this must not be done after the stamp has been mounted. The stamp should be placed loosely on the space intended, pencil marks made in the four corners and then connected, using Indian ink. The stamp is then mounted inside this frame.

Some collections shown in exhibitions have the most elaborate writing-up. Many stamp designs, varieties, errors, watermarks, etc. are illustrated by enlarged drawings and water colour paintings. In many cases, if the ornamentation is done artistically, it is greatly admired and certainly conveys a lot of information. But the collector should bear in mind that too many drawings and too much writing-up inevitably take something from the stamps themselves and the attention is distracted.

Collectors who want to keep " entires "—for instance airmail letters, First Day covers or an envelope with a classic stamp—can use spring-back covers of a convenient size, into which are inserted pages of stout paper or card and the envelopes can be mounted on hinges, one or two to a page. Special albums are on sale, which contain pockets of pellucid paper into which the " entire " can be slipped. The pocket can be turned so that cancellations, arrival postmarks, etc. at the back of the " entire " can also be inspected. With a little skill it is not difficult to make an album for " entires" by using large transparent envelopes fastened to cartridge or drawing paper cut to appropriate size and inserted into a spring-back or peg-system binder.

CHAPTER 6

How Stamps are Made

It is possible to collect stamps without knowing the details of their manufacturing processes. But even the beginner will soon be confronted with errors in the design, varieties such as plate flaws, or differences in the paper, perforation, watermark or colour of stamps seemingly of the same issue. In many cases such varieties make a considerable difference to the value of the stamps. The beginner will ask himself why and how they occur, and he will desire to learn something about the technicalities of stamp production. The advanced collector and specialist who embarks upon the study of stamps will, of course, need much more information.

It starts with the postal authority commissioning an artist, or announcing a competition and inviting several artists to submit designs. The artist is given some specifications, informed about the purpose of the new issue—for instance if it is a stamp or a set of stamps intended to commemorate a famous person or a historical event, he will be asked to draw the portrait of that person or a scene pertaining to the event—and told what figures of value and inscriptions he has to incorporate. He will also be advised about the intended printing process and the colour in which the stamp or stamps will be printed.

The artist produces the design on a scale several times larger than the intended size of the stamp. Usually he completes several designs, which might be printed as " essays," on card and in black only, so that the post office chiefs can examine the effect of the picture and make a final choice. The artist's design is then reduced, usually by photography, to the intended size of the stamp in order to find out whether the drawing and particularly the words and figures will bear reduction to the very small format of a stamp.

PRINTING

The next step is to reproduce the design on the lithographic stone, or to make a " negative " for processing a " clichée," or to transfer it on to a plate or cylinder for recess, photogravure, or rotogravure printing. There are many printing processes and the most important of these are:

Lithography. The design is transferred to the stone or a zinc or aluminium plate by the use of a special ink and " fixed " by treatment with acid. The stone or plate is wetted by moist rollers, the moisture is absorbed by the blank spaces, but rejected by the greasy ink of the lines of the design. In the printing press the ink rollers (carrying the desired dye) rotate over the stone or plate; the ink is repelled by the wet (blank) parts, but adheres to the inked parts. The paper is then inserted and when brought in contact with the stone or plate absorbs the inked parts and an impression is obtained.

Typography or Surface Printing. The primitive form of this process was printing from wood-blocks. In more modern methods the design is cut by an engraver in steel, in relief, and a die is made. The die is then multiplied by stereotyping or electrotyping and plates of copper metal are produced of, say, 100 similar stamp pictures, which are printed on a flat press. The copper plates have surfaces with a layer of harder metal, such as steel, nickel or chromium to give long wear in the printing press.

Line-engraving or Recess Printing. This is a process

opposite to typography in that the design is engraved in reverse on a small plate of steel. This die in recess (also called in French *taille douce*, and in Italian *intaglio*) is multiplied, as in typography. In printing, the ink is dabbed into the recessed lines and the moistened paper brought into contact with the plate picks up the ink lying in the recessed lines. On the finished stamp these coloured lines stand up from the paper surface and can be easily detected when going over the stamp gently with a finger-nail or the tip of a finger.

Printing from Half-tone Clichés. This is a method akin to that used in newspapers to reproduce photographs and advertisement pictures. It is a photo-mechanical method by which clichés, which can be multiplied, are reproduced on sensitive zinc or alloy plates. The design appears in tiny dots or criss-cross lines because a fine screen was interposed between the camera lens and the photographed object. The plate, upon whose sensitive surface the photograph appears, is then etched in acid baths and can be used either in flat press printing or, by a further process, made into cylinders for rotary printing machines.

Offset Printing. This is a modernised method of lithography, in which a zinc or aluminium plate is used instead of the lithographic stone. The plate is made in the form of a bent cylinder and, in a rotary press, inked by rollers, whereupon the pictures are transferred to a second " blanket cylinder," covered with a thin surface of rubber. The stamp pictures appear on this " rubber-sheet " in reverse (negative). The " blanket cylinder " is then brought in contact with the paper and " offsets " the negative picture upon it, so that it appears positive on the paper. It works somewhat like a rubber stamp.

Photogravure. There are many modern methods of this printing process which include rotary gravure (rotogravure) and collotype. The basic method is to reproduce the design by photography on a glass plate, on which it appears as a " negative," then on another glass plate when it becomes a " positive." In photogravure a print is transferred from the second plate on to carbon tissue (paper coated with gelatine) and made sensitive to light. By squeegeeing the carbon tissue to a copper plate the picture is transferred, the carbon tissue is removed and when the copper plate is immersed in acid baths, the design appears upon it. In rotogravure the carbon tissue first has impressed on it a screen consisting of a network of dots or lines, the print is then taken from the glass " positive " and the carbon tissue squeegeed on a copper cylinder, which is then treated as in photogravure. The actual printing process is very similar to that in line-engraved printing.

There are other printing processes in stamp production but those mentioned are, or were, the most frequent. Modern stamps are now produced mainly by recess printing and photogravure or rotogravure.

These modern methods help to prevent forgery for while a forger could fairly easily imitate a stamp printed by lithography or the half-tone method, the forgery of recess printing and photogravure would be uneconomic. A forger can make transfers from a stone, or even run a small flat printing press and use forged clichés, but he will hardly install a rotary press in his parlour.

Before the actual printing starts the printer produces a number of proofs for approval by the post office. Normally such proofs (which might be printed in an entirely different colour from that intended for the stamp) are destroyed, but some find their way to collectors and are coveted by specialists. Similarly, colour proofs are made so that the postal authority can finally decide on the correct hue desired. Such colour proofs are also sought after by specialists.

PAPER AND WATERMARKS

Paper is obviously another important factor in stamp production. In order to protect themselves from forgers, postal authorities use watermarked paper, because it is fairly difficult and costly to produce and unlikely to be forged.

Watermarks are introduced during the manufacture of paper. When the paper pulp is still soft it is pressed between a moving cylinder of wire cloth on which the pattern of the watermark is sewn on. Carefully regulated pressure of the rollers gives just the necessary amount of force to impress the watermark pattern into the still wet paper texture. When the paper sheets dry the watermark remains visible, where the pattern has slightly thinned the paper.

Watermarks are of importance to the stamp collector, as there are many stamps with similar designs printed on differently watermarked paper. This applies particularly to the stamp issues of Great Britain and the British colonies because the Royal Cypher or the C.A. emblem of the Crown Agents have been repeatedly changed. Thus we distinguish between watermarks which show the imperial crown and C.C. (Crown Colony), the crown and C.A. (Crown Agents), multiple crown and C.C., and multiple crown and Script C.A. and so on. Earlier issues of Great Britain have watermarks showing small, medium and large Garter emblems, Single Royal Cypher, Multiple Royal Cypher, as well as Script and Block lettered Royal Cyphers.

It is not possible to describe here all the details of paper manufacture. Paper is made from rags, straw, wood and other bases by a lengthly process of boiling and digesting into pulp.

The philatelist can distinguish between many kinds of

WATERMARKS

1. Medium Garter of Queen Victoria; 2. George VI; 3. Crown CC (Crown Colonies); 4. Crown CA (Crown Agents); 5. Multiple crown CA (first introduced in 1904); 6. Multiple Script CA (introduced in 1921). The following three are German: 7. This was a special watermark used on a 50m. stamp issued in March, 1923; 8. Lozenges (introduced 1905); 9. Swastikas (Hitler régime).

paper and the list is fairly long. Those of importance are:

Batonné, vergé and quadrillé; the first having water-marked lines horizontally or vertically placed parallel at a certain distance apart, the second (also called " laid ") is watermarked with parallel lines close together, crossed at right angles by lines more widely spaced; the last water-marked with cross lines forming squares or oblongs.

Carton is thick paper, usually coated on the surface.

Coated or Surfaced paper is surfaced with a clay or chalk film on its obverse side, and philatelists distin-guish between " enamelled," " chalked " and " glazed " paper.

Coloured paper is one that has been coloured right through during the manufacuring process (for instance " blued paper "), but there are also stamps printed on surface-coloured paper, the reverse side being white.

Dickinson or Silk-thread paper, named after its inventor and originally used for the Mulready envelopes, has tiny silk threads (sometimes in various colours) embedded during the pulp state; the finished product is quite smooth, but the threads are visible.

Granite paper has embedded coloured fibre particles, similar to the silk threads in Dickinson paper.

India and Japanese papers are thin, opaque papers.

Manilla paper is used for envelopes and wrappers, and is a strong paper of coarse texture.

Ordinary paper is a philatelic term used to distinguish it from " coated " or " granite " paper.

Pelure paper is extremely thin and transparent. It has been used sometimes for emergency printings of stamps in war-time, as has been " cigarette " paper.

The use of some of these papers was prompted for security reasons. It is almost impossible to remove postmarks from coated, particularly chalk-surfaced, papers and to use the " cleaned " stamps again. Sometimes specially made papers were ordered by the postal authorities or recommended by printers for particular printing processes, and philatelists talk of " De La Rue," " Jones " and " Cowan " papers used for the production of British and Commonwealth stamps.

Many early stamp issues were printed on several different kinds of paper and the value of these stamps, bearing identical designs, often depends on their paper differences.

GUM

Gum provides another field of interest to the advanced collector. In the early days of stamp production gum was applied to the already printed stamp sheets by brushing it on by hand. Obviously such a primitive method resulted in " varieties," such as stamps with " thick " or " thin " gum, and because different kinds of gum were sometimes used for the same issue, the specialist distinguishes between " thick yellow," " white " and other sorts of gum. Later, gum was applied by machnes, usually before the sheets were printed. Many stamps were, and still are, printed on paper already gummed, but in some modern printing processes ungummed paper (particularly when rotary printing takes place) is used and gum is applied after printing but before perforating. Certain printing processes require that the surface of the already gummed paper is " broken up " before printing into minute sections, by being drawn across " knives "—steel blades set diagonally. A British invention, first used by the London firm of S. Jones & Co., produced a " non-curling gummed paper," the surface of which is broken up in this fashion. If the gum is not closely broken it may show ridges or patterns. Gum-breaker machines sometimes produce such patterns deliberately, described in philately as "riffles", and some modern stamps, particularly those of Germany and Switzerland are printed on "riffled gummed paper." Instead of gum arabic British stamp printers have in recent years used polyvinyl alcohol based gum (PVA), but gum fracturing machines are still used.

In Britain experiments have gone on to devise a method of stamp recognition that would make it possible for lower-paid letters to be segregated by automatic machines instead of by tedious hand processes. The first experiments involved photo-electric cells. Later, metal strips were inserted into the paper and this led to trials with graphite ink and the introduction, at Southampton Head Post Office in 1957, of letter-facing and segregating machines designed to detect " graphite ink " lines on postage stamps. Clearly visible bands of graphite ink—one band on the denomination used for reduced rate postage and two bands on the remainder—were printed on the back of the stamps between the paper and the gum.

Further experiments making use of ultra-violet light to detect bands of phosphor on the face of the stamps proved very successful and the use of graphite lines on the reverse of the stamps was abandoned in 1960, when the first stamps marked only with strips of phosphorescent ink were issued. For some years both plain and phosphor band stamps were manufactured, but since 1967 all British commemorative and pictorial stamps, as well as the ordinary definitive issues below the 2/6 value, have been printed with phosphor bands.

The stamps on lower-paid items, which the Post Office may hold back until other mail has been cleared, are marked with one phosphor band, and the other values with two. The phosphor band, showing up as a matt surface against the shining unmarked portion of the stamp, can usually be detected by looking at the face of the stamp from an oblique angle against a good light.

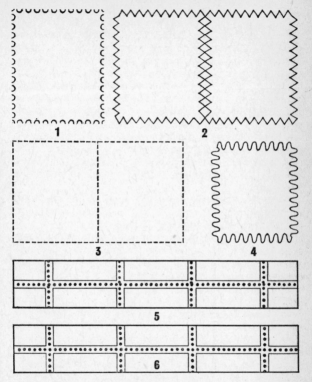

PERFORATIONS

1. Arc rouletting; 2. Zig-zag rouletting; 3. Line rouletting; 4. Serpentine rouletting; 5. Line perforation (note that the corners rarely correspond); 6. Comb or Harrow perforation (the corners are regular)

PERFORATION

In the early days of stamp production the printed and gummed sheets were left imperforate, but soon the postal authorities decided to provide facilities for separating single stamps or panes from sheets when sold to the public. Perforation came into general use after 1855, though the British post office experimented with it as early as 1848.

The precursor of modern perforation was *rouletting*, by which cuts were made between the stamp rows, without any portion of the paper being removed. There are many types of rouletting and those worth mentioning are:

Arc Rouletting (Fr. *Percé en arc*), by which the cuts were made in curved lines. Very fine arc rouletting is called " serrating."

Diamond or Lozenge Rouletting, in which the cuts were made in the shape of little crosses, thus forming diamonds or lozenges at the stamp edges when separated.

Pin Rouletting, by which tiny holes were pricked into the paper of the stamp margins, without any paper being actually removed from the holes. It is sometimes erroneously described as " pin perforation."

Line Rouletting (Fr. *Percé en lignes*), made with straight interrupted cuts.

Rouletting in Colour, when notched, curved metal rules were set between the clichées forming the plate; when the sheets were printed, these rules were inked and slightly cut into the margins of the stamps.

Saw-tooth Rouletting, with cuts made to look like edges of a saw; akin to *Zig-zag Rouletting*.

Serpentine Rouletting, with wavy lines cut between the stamps.

With the advent of perforating machines, rouletting went out, although it has been used, on occasions, as late as in 1919 by Yugoslavia and 1922 by Greece.

Perforation is distinguished from rouletting by holes being punched out from the paper. It can be measured by perforation gauges (see Chapter 4) and the " gauge " is defined by the number of holes (not " teeth ") within a space of 2 centimetres. When we speak of a stamp being perforated $14\frac{1}{2}$, it does not mean that it has either $14\frac{1}{2}$ holes or $14\frac{1}{2}$ teeth, but that the number of holes in this gauge is $14\frac{1}{2}$ on a line 2 centimetres long.

One of the inventors of perforation was an Englishman, Henry Archer. Early perforating machines, some operated by hand, produced various kinds of perforations and the philatelist distinguishes the following as most important:

Single-line Perforation, in which the holes are punched along one straight line, either vertically or horizontally. This was a slow process, as it had to be repeated between each row of stamps down the sheet, which had then to be turned sideways and the operation repeated, the punching now crossing the lines already perforated.

Comb Perforation, by which the pins are arranged in the form of a very wide-toothed comb. The perforator punches the margins at the top and the two sides of the stamps, the sheet moving up and, with the next blow, the perforation of the bottom margin is completed and the two sides of the next row are perforated at the same time.

Harrow Perforation, in which the pins are arranged in rectangles and perforate the whole sheet in one operation.

While normally the perforation is the same on all four sides of a stamp, the distance between the pins or " spurs " being the same, some stamps have " compound perforation," caused when the distance between the pins of the horizontal row is different from the distance between the pins of the vertical row. Thus the " gauge " might be $14\frac{1}{2}$ holes to 2 centimetres horizontally, but $12\frac{1}{2}$ holes to 2

centimetres vertically. We then speak of a stamp being
" perf. 14½ by 12½."

MARGINS

The margins of a stamp sheet are of interest to collectors,
because they bear register marks, control numbers, sometimes dates of the issue, imprints of the printing firm, or
even descriptions of the design. Some collectors specialise
in collecting stamps with marginal pieces, for instance, the
edge with the control number, or *coins datés*, the corner
blocks with the margin bearing the date of issue.

Sometimes in the past, for the convenience of the postal
counter clerks or for reasons of accountancy a few stamps
on the sheet were skipped and replaced by " dummy "
stamps. An example can be found on some early issues
of Austria which were printed in eight rows of eight. In
order to have only 60 accountable stamps on a sheet, the
bottom row had only four " real " stamps and four so
called " St. Andrew's Crosses " showing a white cross on
coloured ground; these pieces had, of course, no postal
validity and were included to make up a round sum of
value for the whole sheet.

COLOUR

A few words must be said about colours. A tremendous
variety of colours occur in stamp production. Dyes of
various chemical substances have been used in the past,
sometimes with disastrous results for collectors. For
instance aniline dyes tend to run, some printing inks fade,
others change their original hue through exposure to
light or humidity, making the stamp into a " changeling."

During printing the ink is fed continuously into the
rollers but the flow (at least in primitive printing processes)

cannot always be completely regulated. When the rollers
are either very well inked, or when they are running rather
dry, the colour of some sheets may be darker or much
lighter than that of the bulk of printing. Collectors
then distinguish " shade varieties," some of which might
be quite rare because only a small quantity of the stamps
exists with very dark or very light hues of the same issue.
Moreover, many stamps of the same design often remain
current for years and are printed in large quantities at
different times; it is not always possible to obtain exactly
the same result as regards the shade, and thus one finds
in catalogues descriptions such as " pale," " light,"
" bright," " dull," " dark," etc. While a stamp appears
to the beginner as being just blue, the specialist might
distinguish between six or more hues of the same " blue "
issue. Colour guides are a help in such cases.

BOOKLETS, TÊTE-BÊCHE, SE-TENANT

Many postal authorities issue stamp booklets, which
contain pages of six, eight or more stamps of different
values. To produce these booklets, the stamps must be
printed in such a way as to provide side margins for the
small pages, so that they can be stapled between the
outside covers. A quantity of sheets is produced with two
or more rows of stamps printed " tête-bêche," that is
" head to foot". When they are separated and bound in
the booklets one cannot trace their original " tête-bêche "
position, but some postal authorities sell to collectors these
special sheets, with the " tête-bêche " rows intact. Blocks
of pairs of such " tête-bêche " stamps are collected as a
philatelic sideline. Some postal authorities even print
stamps of different designs and colour on the same sheet
for inclusion in booklets (particularly Switzerland) and

one can find, for instance, a 5 centimes green together with a 10 centimes red on the same sheet, separated by perforation. Such pairs are called " se-tenant."

RE-ENTRY, DUPLICATION

As already mentioned, various accidents can occur during printing processes and some are of particular importance to the stamp collector, quite apart from plate flaws and minor varieties caused by dirt, scratches and such like.

Such major accidents include " re-entries," " duplications," " double-embossing," etc. A " re-entry " is, strictly speaking, a repair to a worn or damaged cliché or plate and is made after some printing has been carried out. When the transfer roller is used again after the correction has been carried out, it will be almost impossible to discover that a new " entry " has been made. But on many occasions the erasure on the original design is not complete. After the engraver has added a few new lines, some of the old ones remain still visible and a " non-coincident re-entry " results.

A " shifted transfer " is caused by failure of the design on the transfer roller to coincide at the end of its return excursion with the lines pressed on the plate at the begining of its forward journey. This will show on some or all of the stamps on the sheet, particularly at the top, bottom or sides.

" Duplication " can occur on stamps printed by typographic and line-engraved recess processes, for instance by double-striking of the die upon the mould used for reproduction. Some or all lines of the design will then appear double. A similar appearance of the design may result from a duplicated transfer on to a lithographic stone, and this is called a " double transfer."

Some stamps were produced by embossing, that is by stamping in coloured or colourless relief, and when a sheet was put by mistake twice through the embossing machine and the paper slightly shifted, "double embossing" resulted, with the relief or part of it appearing twice on the stamp.

All these accidents produce "varieties" which the specialist eagerly collects.

A VISIT TO A STAMP PRINTER

Members of philatelic clubs are sometimes able to arrange visits to the printing works of some of the large stamp printers. The beginner as well as the advanced philatelist will be well advised to make use of such an opportunity. During the past hundred years British and most British Empire stamps were produced by five famous printing firms, Perkins, Bacon & Co., De La Rue & Co., Harrison & Sons, Waterlow & Sons, and Bradbury, Wilkinson & Co.

British and British Commonwealth stamps are very popular among collectors all over the world. They are usually extremely attractive and very well printed. The British public uses about 8,000 million postage stamps a year and this means that over 600 million stamps are printed every month, or more than 30 million every working day. Some 18,000 million stamps for overseas postal administration are also printed each year in Britain, a not unimportant addition to our export trade.

One of the large stamp printers, at High Wycombe in Buckinghamshire, produce not only most of the British and Commonwealth stamps but also print stamps for many foreign postal authorities. Tucked away out of the track of prying eyes and well guarded by security officers stand the modern buildings of these printing works. It is always summer in the stamp printing departments; a temperature around 70° F. is maintained and the humidity of the air is carefully controlled by air-conditioning apparatus. Unless the special paper is kept at the same temperature and humidity throughout all operations, printing, gumming and perforating, there would be stretching, contraction or curling and the impression and perforation would be inaccurate.

Every piece of the special paper used is checked and scrap —whether printer's waste or trimmings—must be accounted for and destroyed under control of G.P.O. inspectors. This is one of the measures to prevent counterfeiting.

In the printing process thousands of gallons of the finest ink, specially mixed to maintain exactly the same hue for years, are used to feed the ink rollers.

When the printing is completed, the paper is passed through the cutting and perforating machines. Special sheets are printed for coils to be used in slot machines and for the production of stamp booklets, while " ordinary " sheets are usually separated to contain 240 stamps each.

Every sheet passes the scrutiny of inspectors, mostly women, who have an uncanny gift of discovering printing flaws—to the disappointment of collectors. So rare are oversights that modern British stamps with the tiniest flaw or missed perforation command very high prices as rare philatelic varieties, for instance, the G.B. (S.G. 624) Post Office Savings Bank Centenary 1961, 3d. stamp, with orange colour missing.

After several other checks the stamp sheets are packed into bundles and dispatched to the G.P.O. where they are stored and distributed to thousands of post offices. During all the operations G.P.O. inspectors are on duty and a final check is made before the stamps reach the counter.

CHAPTER 7

Some Puzzles to Solve

When sorting stamps out of a large packet bought in a stamp shop or from a shoe box acquired at a stamp auction, or when going through an " office lot," presented by a friend or kind uncle who works in a large business firm, the new recruit to philately may encounter some seemingly insoluble puzzles.

Most of the stamps he will be able to identify quickly as having been issued by this or that country, because on the majority of modern issues the name of the country is included in the design. Obviously, the country's name is in her own language, but one will discover without much trouble that " ESPAÑA " means Spain, or " DEUTSCHE BUNDES REPUBLIK " denotes German Federal Republic. A dictionary can be consulted and in this way the beginner will discover that Austria is called "ÖSTER-REICH " in the language of that country and that " BEL-GIQUE " means Belgium.

But many stamps have no such easy indications. The beginner will soon admit defeat when faced with inscriptions in a foreign alphabet—Chinese, Japanese, Cyrillic or Arabic. Even if some inscriptions are in Latin characters, he will discover that the name of the country has been omitted and that the inscription only gives the face value and the word " Postage " or such like.

Indeed, the British G.P.O. is guilty of just this omission. Place yourself for a moment in the position of a philatelic recruit in some foreign country, looking at his first British stamp. He will find no indication of the origin of any

British stamp issued during the reigns of six sovereigns, from Queen Victoria to Queen Elizabeth II. On the postage stamps of Great Britain there are printed only the words " Postage " and " Revenue," the face value and sometimes the initials or cypher of the reigning Queen or King. However, there will be very few who will not recognise the portraits of the Queen and her predecessors.

Admittedly, it is easier for a foreigner to recognise a British stamp than for us to identify many foreign ones. The beginner will have, therefore, to sort stamps of puzzling origin into some general groups. Everybody will distinguish between, say, Chinese and Cyrillic characters, the latter much resembling our own. The sorting will start by putting all stamps suspected of coming from the Far East into one tray, those with apparently Arabic inscriptions into another and those with seemingly Russian characters into a third and so on.

Let's take the Far Eastern tray first. The stamps could be from China, Japan, Siam, Manchuria, Nepal, Korea or some of the former Indian States. Now, there will be a few clues to follow. A chrysanthemum will point to Japan, dragon designs on the early stamps of China will provide a clue to that country, while on her modern issues the portraits of President Sun-Yat-Sen, General Chiang Kai-Shek and President Mao Tse-Tung will be helpful to those collectors who may have seen their pictures in a book or newspaper.

Then, looking through the catalogue and comparing the illustrations of Chinese, Japanese, Siamese or Nepalese stamps, the collector will find certain similarities or differences in the strangely scrawled characters and finally identify not only the country but the stamp in question. The large Stanley Gibbons catalogues contain many thousands of illustrations and all the " difficult " stamps are depicted.

Stamps with Arabic characters might come from Turkey, any of the Middle East countries, Persia, Afghanistan or some of the Indian States. The crescent and star, originally used only by Turkey and Egypt, have been adopted by other Moslem countries, but fortunately Pakistan, while using this emblem and Arabic inscriptions, also adds its name in English, as do all the other Asiatic and African members of the British Commonwealth, as well as Iraq, Persia (Iran) and Israel, the latter in addition to Arabic and Hebrew inscriptions. Again with the help of the catalogue, after some initial sorting, the stamps will be properly identified.

Cyrillic characters will suggest to us that the stamp comes from Russia, Serbia, Yugoslavia, Montenegro, Bulgaria or Greece. The Cyrillic alphabet is similar in the first five instances and slightly different in the Greek language. As several letters of the Cyrillic and Latin alphabet are similar, a little guesswork will help, and " CPBNJA " might be not too difficult to unravel as meaning " Serbia ".

Portraits of the Russian Tsars, Lenin, Stalin and Tito will be easily recognised, and most Yugoslav stamps bear the name of the country also in Latin characters, as the Croats and Slovenes, who represent a large part of the population, do not use the Cyrillic alphabet.

Indeed, some of the inscriptions in our own alphabet may cause more trouble than those in foreign characters. What, for instance, means " MAGYARORSZAG "? Some people will know that a " Magyar " is a Hungarian, and rightly deduct that it means " Hungary " and that " MAGYAR POSTA " denotes " Hungarian Post." On some early stamps of Spain there is only the word " CORREOS," which means " Posts " and the same applies to some of the early issues of South American republics.

Where the country is not named or is hidden behind a name which is not similar to that used in English, the word indicating the currency will give a clue. Thus, for example, the word " peseta " or " peso " will indicate either Spain or a Spanish-speaking South American country. A beginner will do well to compile a list of all world currencies, their names can be found in many reference books, including *Whitaker's Almanack*, which can be consulted in every public library.

Quite apart from any language difficulties the collector may experience, there will be other puzzles to solve. There are quite a number of early stamps which bear no inscriptions whatsoever, apart from a numeral. Among them are the " Bull's-eyes " of Brazil, which was one of the first countries to issue stamps, in 1843, and several of her later issues until 1866. The early stamps of Persia show a lion and the figure of value (in Arabic) but nothing else. Some of the stamps of Egypt issued in 1867 have only the initials P.E. (Postes Egyptiennes) in the corners, but here of course the picture of the Sphinx provides an immediate identification.

Even in modern times there are such " dumb " stamps from European countries. All postage due issues of Switzerland from 1878 to 1924 bore only a numeral, or a numeral with the white cross of the Confederation. Their design showing snow covered mountain peaks will facilitate a good guess. Incidentally, nearly all Swiss stamps bear the inscription " HELVETIA," her ancient Latin name, because the Swiss population is either German, French, Italian or Rhaeto-Romanic speaking and it is too cumbersome to include inscriptions in four languages within the space of a small stamp.

Mere identification of stamps according to their country of origin is, however, only the start on the road to philately. There are a great many stamps which will look similar to

76

the new recruit and yet have minute differences in the design and will have been issued at different times. The ability to recognise stamps is one of the great satisfactions of the hobby. The collector will have to learn to use his eyes, and the catalogue will be a never-ending source of new discoveries.

Only a few examples can be given here. The first adhesive stamp, the Penny Black of Great Britain, was printed from line-engraved plates. The plates were not numbered, although experts can to-day distinguish them by subtle differences in engraving. Altogether eleven different plates were used and their numbers were printed on the margins of the sheets. Many more plates were used for the 1d. red of 1841-57. Then, in 1858, a slightly altered design was introduced, with " control letters " in all four corners, and on these stamps, until the last printing in 1864, the plate numbers were indicated in the design, in the frame ornaments on both sides. The numbers run from 71 to 225. They are fairly easily seen, if the stamps are not too heavily postmarked. The work of detecting them is fascinating, considering that the stamps printed from certain plates are now great rarities. While, for instance, stamps with the plate numbers 120, 122, 140, 152, 174, 183, 198, 204, 205, 206, 208, 209 are very common and worth only a few pence, those bearing Nos. 83, 132, 219, 223, 224 are valued between 10/- and 25/- each, No. 225 is quite rare and worth about £10, and No. 77 is a rarity most difficult to come by and valued at up to £2000. Many other plate numbers range in value from 1/- to 5/- each. All these prices are for used specimens, and mint stamps of these issues are much more valuable.

Another example of a small difference in the design is the 1d. lilac of Great Britain, issued in 1881. It shows the portrait of Queen Victoria in a frame which has small pearls in each of the four corners. These stamps were surface printed and two dies were prepared. In Die I there are 14 pearls in each corner, but Die II shows 16 pearls. Stamps printed from Die I are worth about 8/- each, while the second issue is quite common.

The 1d. red of Australia, issued in 1913, shows the portrait of King George V, flanked by a kangaroo and an emu. One year later this plate was redrawn and the design more clearly etched, especially in the shading of the King's face and the pictures of the two animals. The earlier stamps are worth much more, because a much smaller printing was made than of those subsequently issued. The recognition of the two issues will, however, be easy even for the beginner, because the first issue was printed on unwatermarked paper, while for the second paper a watermark showing an " A " surmounted by a crown was used. Again, there are some further differences in the design of the second issue, particularly in regard to the figure " 1," but such minute differences will only be of interest to a collector who specialises in the stamps of Australia.

There are many slight differences in the designs of stamps of every country caused by technical improvements or re-making of plates and dies for subsequent printings of the same stamp. In some cases changes in design have been made deliberately for good reasons, apart from those caused by improved printing methods.

Most British Colonial issues prior to pictorial designs— particularly during the reigns of Queen Victoria, King Edward VII, and King George V—were in the so called " Colonial key type." The designs were similar for many colonies and the names of the colonies and protectorates were inserted in black or colour. There are two main dies of the " key type," showing infinitesimal differences in the frame ornaments. For instance, in the " Georgian key type " the background of the words Postage and Revenue has square top corners in Die I, but the corners are curved in Die II. All this is carefully described and illustrated in the large catalogues and, while the differences seem unimportant, they affect the value of the stamps of the two dies.

A good example of a re-drawn design are the " chain breaker " stamps of Yugoslavia of 1918. In one of the designs the chain is shorter and does not touch the frame, in others the chain is longer, reaching down to the frame. When, in 1867, a set was issued by Austria depicting the be-whiskered Emperor Francis Joseph, his beard and moustache were drawn in coarse, thick lines. It is said the Emperor did not like this and in 1874 the same stamps were issued with his whiskers redrawn and looking more silky and soft.

Norwegian stamps between 1871 and 1922 had a similar design: a posthorn surmounted by the royal crown. But in the course of half a century this design was repeatedly re-drawn and the posthorn as well as the frame and figures or value later appeared with different shadings and were much cleaner and clearer.

The 1906 issue of France, the so-called " Sower " type, shows Marianne standing on a piece of soil and busily scattering seed. A later re-drawn design, while retaining the picture, deprived Marianne of that small piece of land.

When a new pictorial set was issued for Fiji, bearing the portrait of King George VI, the artist drew for the 1½d. stamp the picture of a native canoe, floating far from the shore. Soon the Post Office was receiving many sarcastic letters, asking how the canoe could sail as far away without anyone aboard. So it was decided to re-draw the stamp and put a tiny figure of a native into the boat. The originally issued stamp was withdrawn after a short while and replaced by a new one which, apart from the boatman, was identical with the first one. Now the stamp with the unmanned boat is worth about 10/- while the redrawn stamp is catalogued at a mere 2/-.

Stamps of Transvaal of 1894-96 have the Boer Republic's coat of arms, in which is included the picture of a trek wagon. The artist drew the wagon with two shafts, but when many people protested that the traditional wagon had only one shaft, the *dissel-boom*, the stamps were redrawn and the wagon shown as it was really used by the Boers.

When the Russian Imperial Post Office issued, in 1891, a set of stamps for Finland, which was then a Russian province, these stamps seemed at first glance to be exactly similar to the contemporary Russian stamps. But, for those printed for use in the Finnish province, the design was slightly altered by including small circles in the background.

Thus two stamps which appear to the beginner as being similar because they bear the same, or seemingly the same, design can be very different, and there may also be considerable difference in their relative value. Needless to say these differences apply not only to slight changes in the design, but even more so to different paper, watermarks and perforations. There are many stamps printed from the same plate or die which are identical in their designs, but because they have different watermarks or were perforated by different machines they are regarded by the philatelist as different stamps. Ascertaining and classifying such differences provides one of the main interests of philately.

EARLY GREAT BRITAIN

Top: The £1 brown-lilac of 1881-8. *Second Row:* A margin
pair of the first 2d. blue of 1840, showing the same design as the
Penny Black, engraved by Frederick Heath; and the 10s. ultra-
marine of 1883-4. *Bottom row:* The first perforated stamp, a 1d.
red of 1854-7; and one of the three embossed stamps engraved
at the Royal Mint, the 10d. brown of 1848-54.

SOME RARE CLASSICS

From left to right: A 5 c. stamp issued by the Swiss Canton of
Geneva in 1845; one of the first perforated stamps of Brazil, a
430 reis of 1866; the " Bâle Dove," issued by the Swiss Canton of
Bâle in 1845; a 5 c. " Poste Locale " issued by the Swiss Canton of
Neuchâtel; the first stamp of Sweden, a 3 Skilling value; one of
the earlier stamps of Roumania, a 50 Bani of 1869. *Below:* A rare
unused pair of the 1 franc of the French Empire of 1853; and
one of the first stamps of the Italian States, a 50 grana of Naples,
1858.

CHAPTER 8

Varieties, Errors and Forgeries

VARIETIES

Once the beginner has learned to recognise stamps and has realised that he must use his eyes (as well as a magnifying glass, a catalogue and some other " tools ") to distinguish differences in the designs and other characteristics, he will be well on the road to embarking on the study of " varieties."

What is a variety? This word is used loosely (and often wrongly) and has several meanings. In philately a " variety " can mean, generally, a stamp. We speak of a " variety packet " as one containing a number of different stamps. More exactly, a variety is a stamp which is not a " normal " one and shows some characteristics not common to the majority of stamps of the same issue. A stamp printed from Die II of the Colonial key type (mentioned in the previous chapter) is not a variety of Die I. It is a normal stamp belonging to another re-drawn issue. But, if a stamp of the Colonial key type printed from Die II has a flaw, which the majority of the stamps of that issue have not, then it is a variety of the Die II issue.

Thus, a " variety " is a stamp which differs in some small way from the standard stamp of its own issue.

Most varieties are caused by some technical hitch during the preparation of a lithographic stone, the engraving of a plate, the processing of a block and, more often, during the printing process.

When stamps were produced by lithography, the artist had to draw each on the sheet by hand. Each drawing might have differed very slightly from the other but this would not make each a variety. But if the artist made a spelling mistake on one of his drawings, then this stamp would be a variety and would appear only once on each sheet printed from the same stone.

If during printing a tiny speck of dirt settles on the plate and the printer does not sweep it off, then many sheets might be produced with one stamp showing a dark or a colourless blot, because either a surfeit of ink had accumulated on the tiny foreign body, or the speck prevented the ink reaching the paper. This, obviously, would occur only once on a sheet of, say, a hundred stamps. Ninety-nine will be " normal," the one with the blot will become a variety and, if only a limited printing of the issue was made, even a rarity, because only a small number of the variety ever reached the post office counter. Moreover, because most people who bought such a stamp to put on a letter, or received a letter with such a variety never realised any difference in its appearance, a large proportion of varieties have been thrown away and lost to collectors. Thus, there are varieties which exist only in very small numbers and this makes them rarities.

On the other hand, if several million sheets of a new stamp were printed and issued and the variety occurs once on every sheet, then there might be quite a large number of these varieties about. Collectors, dealers and editors of philatelic journals carefully inspect every new issue—dealers having the additional advantage of buying several sheets of every new stamp. They will be quick in discovering the variety. In this case, the variety, though much higher priced than the normal stamp of the same issue, will not necessarily become a rarity.

The most notable varieties are stamps with inverted

centres. They were caused before the introduction of more modern printing methods, during printing by the flat-bed process, using blocks. When a stamp was printed in two colours, the coloured centre design was printed in one operation and the, let's say, black frame design in a second. It happened that a sheet was inserted into the printing press the wrong way for the second impression and the centre design was, therefore, " inverted."

British and British Colonial stamps have always been printed with great efficiency and there are only a few such flagrant varieties with inverted centres. Here is a short list of British Commonwealth " inverts ":

Tonga, 1897, 7½d. black and green.
Labuan, 1901, 8 cents, postage due.
New Zealand, 1903, 4d. blue and brown.
Cook Islands, 1920, 1d. carmine and black.
Jamaica, 1920, 1s. orange-yellow and red-orange.
Charkari (Indian State), 1931, 5 rupees, turquoise and
    purple.
Cook Islands, 1932, 1d. lake and black.
Cook Islands, 1932, 2d. brown and black.
Canada, 1960, 5c. St. Lawrence Seaway commemorative.

The most famous British colonial stamp with an inverted centre is that of India, issued in 1854, a 4 annas, blue and red, with the head of Queen Victoria upside down. Only sixteen copies of this variety are known to exist and when one was offered for sale recently, it changed hands for a price of several thousand pounds.

Another exceptional " invert " is the 4d. stamp of Western Australia of 1854. It was printed in one colour only, blue, the printing process thus not requiring two operations which caused all the other " inverts." The stamp was, however, printed from a lithographic stone, and the centre design showing a swan was put " topsy
83

turvy " on the stone when the transfer, made in two parts, was laid down.

There exists a fairly large number of foreign " inverts." Some of the numeral issues of Denmark between 1870 and 1904 which were printed in two colours have almost as many inverted frames as normal ones and most of these varieties are quite common. One of the most famous foreign " inverts " is the 24 cents airmail stamp of the United States of 1918, with the aircraft flying upside down. Spain, Russia, some French and Portuguese colonies and quite a number of South American countries have their " inverts." In some cases the suspicion that some of these varieties were not altogether accidental, but produced with an eye on stamp collectors, cannot be entirely discounted.

Inversion can, obviously, occur quite frequently when a stamp is overprinted. It only needs the sheet to be fed the wrong way round into the press to make the overprint stand on its head.

Overprints provide a multitude of varieties. They are produced, as a rule, in a hurry and if a stamp had to be surcharged with another value the figures were sometimes set by a compositor from different types. Thus, as in our illustration (p. 85), on the same sheet there appeared a " 50 " in several sizes or varied thicknesses and the same issue provided many varieties.

A good example are the " Decimal " overprints of Pakistan, Basutoland, Bechuanaland and Swaziland, all produced locally and in a great hurry. Pakistan had a bad record in 1947 when, after the proclamation of her independence, stamps of India were overprinted with " PAKISTAN," the overprint having been made both by machine printing and by hand-stamping, in various types, sizes and colours. When the " Paisa " decimal currency was introduced in 1961, six values were overprinted and the printers at Karachi, unable to cope with the entire printing, employed sub-contractors. This resulted in a number of different types, varying in character and length, being used and also in the production of many varieties, including misprints, such as " PASIA " for " Paisa." Moreover, many stamps were overprinted by local postmasters by " hand-stamping " the values of the new currency.

The stamps of the three British protectorates in South Africa were overprinted with the decimal values at the South African Government Printing Works in Pretoria.

25c   **25c**   **25c**

Tempo Bold.   Tempo Medium.   Tempo Bold Condensed.

50   **50**   **50**   **50**   **50**

Pf.   Pf.   Pf.   Pf.   Pf.

OVERPRINTS

The top row shows three different varieties of type used by the printers on stamps of Basutoland, Bechuanaland and Swaziland when the change-over to decimal currency took place in 1961. The row below shows different varieties of the 50 Pfennig overprint on some German stamps.

After the first consignment was delivered, the printers distributed the type and when they were subsequently asked for further supplies, the overprints had to be re-set. The result was that the new overprints greatly differed from those of the first issue. Three different kinds of " Tempo " type were in fact used, as well as " Bodoni ".

Double prints happen sometimes when an already printed sheet is fed once again into the press and, because of a slight shifting of the paper, the design appears twice. But the collector must beware of mixing up a " double print " with " printer's waste." Printers often insert an already printed sheet again to check up on the depth of colour or the clearness of the impression; this " waste " is thrown away but sometimes finds its way to collectors.

Another kind of variety occurs when there is incomplete printing. As I mentioned, in the British Colonial key types the names of the colonies were inserted in a separate printing operation, and there exist a number of varieties with the name omitted.

Some varieties are almost unbelievable. It happened that a sheet already printed on the face side was inserted again and printed on the reverse side. As the paper is often gummed before printing, the second printing was made on the gum. In the case of a stamp of Venezuela, a 25 centimos sheet already printed was fed into the press again when the 5 c. value was being produced. This resulted in a sheet having the 25c. on the face and the 5c. on the reverse side. Such a " double " stamp is worth today about £25, while normally the 5c. and 25c. values are catalogued at 1/-.

Another wide field of varieties is provided by colour differences. When a stamp is current for a long time and a number of printings are made, it is obvious that the ink used may differ on various occasions. It is not a colour change, which is made deliberately by order of the Post Office (for instance to comply with the international rules laid down by the Universal Postal Union) but a " shade variety." Many stamps have different shades and a stamp described officially by the issuing postal authority as " red " may exist in hues from deep carmine to light pink.

The beginner, discovering that two similar stamps have different perforations, may jump to the conclusion that one of them is a variety. But differences in perforation do not always make a variety. Indeed, for technical reasons, for instance because of the installation of a new, improved perforating machine, the same stamp may have two or more different perforations during its currency. This is the case with many British colonial stamps, particularly of the George VI issues. Some are perforated 13½, others 14, others again 13½ by 14 and so on.

A perforation variety is one where the unusual perforation occurred through a mistake and not by the deliberate change of the perforation machine.

The same applies to watermarks. The beginner may find that two stamps of a similar design and colour have two different watermarks. The reason for this is that the watermark had been deliberately changed during the currency of the stamp, and at a subsequent printing paper with a new watermark was used. A watermark variety can, however, occur if, for instance, the paper is inserted the wrong way round, and the watermark then appears "inverted," though this may be "normal" in the production of stamps for booklets and coils for coin machines.

A stamp issued perforated may be found imperforate. Such a variety is caused by oversight in putting a sheet through the perforating machine after it has been printed. Printers working for the British post office carefully check every sheet leaving their works and the G.P.O. employs inspectors, who once again examine every sheet received before distribution to the post office counters. However, on rare occasions, an imperforated sheet does slip through and an ordinary 3d. stamp of a current issue without perforation becomes a rarity.

In addition to such obvious varieties as some of the examples described there are thousands of minor ones, which are of interest to the specialist but should be disregarded by the beginner. There is hardly any issue, whatever its printing process, in which some kind of variety could not be found. But the beginner and, indeed, also the advanced collector, should beware of " fly speck philately."

Modern stamps are now nearly always produced by photo-mechanical processes, photogravure, or roto-gravure, which leave little to the collector in the way of varieties caused by printing.

When a whole reel of paper is put on to a rotary press and millions of stamp sheets are produced as quickly as a newspaper, there is hardly any chance of double prints, inverted watermarks and such like. Similarly, if a roto-gravure cylinder is made for several complete sheets, no bits and pieces, single clichés, or letters can fall out, and no inverted centres or frames occur.

All that can happen is a minute scratch, a tiny bruise on the surface of the cylinder or plate, or a dust speck causing a small dot. This is quickly corrected and even if a few " fly speck varieties " are produced, they are of little philatelic significance, unless perhaps to the particularly pedantic specialist.

Confronted with the multitude of " real " varieties of many kinds caused by antiquated printing processes in the past, the collector will be well advised to turn his back on " fly-speck " hunting. Indeed, he might come to the rash conclusion that, because of the existence of many varieties in early stamp issues, " serious " philately is nowadays not only beyond his purse and his opportunities of leisure, but also beyond his ability to detect the complexities.

But such fears are without foundation. One of the attractions of our hobby is that it leaves the amateur free to make up his own mind how and what to collect. It is not given to everyone of us to become a philatelic expert or a " great specialist." But a cricketer can thoroughly enjoy a game on the village green without ever aspiring to appear in a Test Match; and exactly the same applies to the collector who can derive much pleasure from collecting without becoming a " variety fiend."

ERRORS

The philatelic term "variety" is sometimes quite wrongly applied to errors made by an artist when designing a stamp. A few examples will make the difference between these two terms obvious.

The Greek post office issued in 1927 a set commemorating the centenary of the Greek War of Independence. One of the stamps had a portrait of the British admiral, Sir Edward Codrington, who commanded the combined British, French and Russian sea forces assisting the Greeks against the Turks. The Greek artist who designed the stamp included an inscription beneath the portrait which read "Sir Codrington," being unaware of the British custom that the Christian name must always follow the title of knighthood. The error was hurriedly corrected by the issue of a new stamp, quite similar in every aspect, but with the correct inscription "Sir Edward Codrington." The second stamp is, of course, not a variety of the first one, but a new stamp in its own right.

A very similar mistake was made by the famous French stamp designer H. Cheffer who prepared the picture for the commemorative issued for the 300th anniversary of the publication of a book by the philosopher Descartes. The inscription flanking Descartes' portrait read *Discours sur la méthode*, but the correct title of the philosopher's great work was *Discours de la méthode*. The French post office withdrew the wrongly captioned stamp and replaced it by an exactly similar one, but with the book title corrected. Again, the first stamp represents an error and neither of the two stamps is a variety.

The picture of a building on the 4d. value of the 1957 issue of Pitcairn Island had a caption "Pitcairn School." But, in fact, the building was the Schoolteacher's House and the stamp was withdrawn and replaced by one of a similar design but with the correct caption.

On some German stamps of the inflation period of 1921, the design shows a miner handling his pick with his left arm. When later the same design was re-issued for different values the picture was reversed and the miner was now holding the pick in his right hand.

Errors like that occur from time to time and are not always limited to the design. The 5d. stamp of Fiji, which appeared in 1938, was printed in blue and scarlet. The colours were approved by the Crown Agents. The picture showed a sugar cane plantation and the plants appeared in bright blue. Many people were soon asking the Fiji postal authorities since when sugar cane had been blue. The stamp was withdrawn after a short circulation and replaced by one in altered colours—green and scarlet. The sugar cane now appeared in its natural green colour to the satisfaction of all. The first issued stamp in the wrong colour is now valued at over £2 while its corrected successor has the modest catalogue value of only 2/6.

Errors in overprints which are frequently prepared in haste, are quite numerous. An amusing overprint error appeared on the total printing of a stamp issued for the New Zealand Protectorate of Niue in 1903. Before the issue of its own stamps Niue used New Zealand stamps with an appropriate overprint and on this occasion the 1s. stamp was to be overprinted with the words " Taha e Sileni," which means in the Kanaka dialect " one shilling." But, instead, the overprint read " Tahae Sileni." The " e " had just slipped a little to the left. The word " Tahae " stands in Kanaka for " thief " and the overprint now meant " shilling thief ". The " thief " stamp was withdrawn and replaced by one with the correct spelling. The error is catalogued now at more than £20, while the corrected stamp is valued at only 25s.

FORGERIES

Apart from varieties and errors the collector may occasionally come across forged or faked stamps. The study of this field of philately is best left to the expert and there are Expert Committees whose members specialise in the scientific examination of rare stamps and the detection of forgeries

Not many years after the first stamps appeared, forgers turned their attention to them. In some way stamps were " money," like bank notes, and counterfeiting could be quite profitable. The first stamp forgeries were made entirely at the expense of postal authorities. Stamps were forged in order to sell them to the public at face value, in the same way as forged banknotes are put into circulation. Very soon, however, forgers realised that a much more profitable and far less dangerous business was to produce stamp forgeries for sale to collectors. We have, therefore, to distinguish between forgeries made to defraud a post office and those to cheat philatelists.

With one famous exception (the Stock Exchange stamp forgery, the story of which is told in Chapter 13) Britain was never a successful hunting ground for forgers, because until quite recently stamps were sold exclusively at post offices. But in many other countries stamps could always be bought in all sorts of shops, tobacconists, stationers, grocers and in bars and cafés. Forgers who printed stamps to defraud the postal authorities flourished particularly in Spain, Italy and other countries where counterfeiting of banknotes was regarded in the 19th century as almost a respectable profession. Before Italy was united in 1864, each of the small kingdoms and principalities such as

Modena, Parma, Naples, Romagna, Sardinia, Sicily, Tuscany and the Papal State, issued their own stamps and many of these were forged, as were some of the stamps of the German States which existed before the creation of the German Empire in 1870.

Governments, anxious to eliminate this sort of fraud, took measures against counterfeiters. Stocks of shop-keepers who sold stamps were examined from time to time. By introducing secret marks in the designs of stamps and by using watermarked paper and more elaborate printing methods the production of fraudulent imitations was curtailed, although the forgers succeeded in copying even some of the security devices.

Most of these forgeries concern early issues and a fair number of the forgeries were actually postally used without being detected. Some of the early forgeries are now rare, and specialists collect them and are prepared to pay high prices for them.

With the progress of philately, forgers turned their attention to collectors. Most European governments took a lenient view of this sort of counterfeiting. Forging of stamps which had been withdrawn from circulation and were thus of no further interest to postal authorities was not regarded as a criminal offence and collectors received no protection from the law. At the end of the nineteenth century there were many forgers' workshops in Paris and throughout Germany which produced so-called " rare " stamps and there were plenty of unscrupulous stamp dealers to handle them.

In most instances the forgeries were crudely produced and sold in complete sheets to middlemen. But some extremely elaborate forgeries were also made and in some cases even postal authorities sold or lent genuine plates and lithographic stones to the " imitators." Such forgeries are extremely difficult to detect. Only the paper and ink which, of course, differed from the materials used in the original printings, provide a clue for the experts.

In some cases the forgers employed very elaborate methods. Early Russian and Finnish stamps were printed on sheets with very wide margins. Forgers acquired parts of genuine sheets and then, using forged dies, printed from them " new " stamps on the margins of the original watermarked paper, thus making the forgeries almost indistinguishable from the genuine article.

In the case of early stamps of Japan, produced by Japanese forgers, respect for the Emperor has helped to make detection easy. These stamps bear the imperial symbol of the chrysanthemum flower. The genuine design shows sixteen petals of the flower. The Japanese forgers did not dare to imitate it because it would have been an insult to the Son of Heaven. Therefore they made the number of petals smaller or larger. The chrysanthemums on the forged stamps have thirteen, fourteen, fifteen, seventeen, eighteen or nineteen petals, but never the proper number of sixteen.

One of the most famous forgers was the late Jean de Sperati, who continued his handiwork until after the last war. He was responsible for some excellent forgeries of the rare stamps of France, Switzerland, Spain, the German states, Sweden (including the " rarest stamp in the world," the 3 skilling yellow of 1855), and of many British colonial rarities. Sperati used, in many instances, genuine paper, or even genuine stamps, forging only the overprints upon them or adding forgeries to genuine stamps on old envelopes, faking additional postmarks. It was not until 1948 that he was apprehended and convicted for fraud in two sensational trials.

Stamps were also forged by government departments, both during the First and the Second World Wars. The Allies forged German and Austrian stamps in 1914-18, and German and French stamps during the last war, while the Germans produced forgeries of British and Allied stamps. These forgeries were made to supply secret agents dropped in enemy territories and also for other " cloak and dagger " work. They are, of course, of great interest to philatelic specialists, particularly when found on genuine letters conveyed by the unsuspecting postal authorities of the belligerent countries.

FAKES

While forgeries are stamps which have been forged in their entirety, the term " fake " is applied in philately to fraudulent machination by which a genuine stamp is tampered with, for instance in order to produce a " variety."

Stamps with inverted centres were very cleverly faked. The forger bought some sheets of a genuine stamp of which an inverted centre variety exists. The centres of the " normal " stamps were cut out and replaced upside down. By spreading a minute film of paper pulp and regumming the fakes, they became almost indistinguishable from a true " invert."

Another kind of cunning trickery was employed, e.g. on the 1 cent stamp issued by Canada on the occasion of the Silver Jubilee of King George V. This stamp shows a portrait of the king's grand-daughter, Princess Elizabeth, our present Queen. Because of a technical accident every 21st stamp on a block of 100 printed from the first plate shows a little coloured dot under the eye of the princess. Only 8,000 stamps had this little flaw, which is known as the " Weeping Princess." Forgers bought at post offices large quantities of the genuine stamp for 1 cent each and manufactured the little dot upon them. As the genuine variety is now valued at about £10 each, the profit was very handsome. The vigilance of philatelic experts and journalists did, however, prevent any wide sale of the fakes.

Genuine stamps have frequently been used as the raw material for a fraud. For example the 50 cent green and carmine of the Straits Settlements King Edward VII set of 1902 is a fairly common stamp. One day fakers erased the top panel bearing the inscription " Straits Settlements " and the " 50 cents. " at the bottom of the stamp and substituted a handpress printing of " Northern Nigeria " and " £25 " in the empty space. The original stamp cost the fakers a few shillings, while the Northern Nigeria stamp is now catalogued at £6000 and is a famous rarity. Both stamps had identical designs and colours but a difference in the watermarks gave the game away.

Overprints obviously lend themselves to faking. Often the overprinted stamp is much more valuable than its precursor without the overprint, and fakers bought up sheets of the genuine issues and manufactured the overprint upon them.

Varieties of perforation provide another field for producing fakes. As we have seen, a sheet sometimes escapes the perforating machine and the few imperforate specimens of a normally perforated issue represent rare varieties. By removing the perforation " teeth " a fake can be produced. Again, some imperforate stamps, as for instance some early French issues, were privately perforated and these are rare if genuine. Forgers have turned the cheaper imperforate specimens into perforated ones by adding faked perforations.

Sometimes mint stamps are less valuable than cancelled, and here forgers produce faked postmarks and manufacture even complete " entires." There are many specialists who collect rare postmarks and among them forgers still find their victims.

A few words of warning and consolation must be added

for the beginner. First, do not be tempted by offers of rare and valuable stamps at "ridiculous bargain prices." No respectable dealer will give a rare stamp away for nothing or next to nothing. As in the case of diamonds there is a market price for rare stamps. If a diamond ring is offered at a fraction of its usual price, every sensible person will realise that the "diamond" is either paste, or has a very bad flaw, or was stolen. The same applies to rare stamps.

On the other hand, a beginner will be in little danger of acquiring forgeries for good money, because he will have no ambition to go for rarities during the initial period of collecting. Later he will gain sufficient knowledge to be on his guard. Study of the catalogues, handbooks on forgeries, and the philatelic journals, attendance at club lectures and visits to exhibitions will equip him with the knowledge and experience necessary to recognise at least crude forgeries.

Before acquiring a valuable stamp, the collector will demand to be shown a certificate. As already mentioned, the Royal Philatelic Society, the British Philatelic Association and several leading philatelic organisations and experts abroad examine rare stamps for a small fee and issue a certificate with a photograph and description of the stamp submitted, if it is a genuine specimen. Reputable dealers and stamp auctioneers offer all rare stamps with such certificates, which provide a guarantee of genuineness and can be used when the collector wishes to dispose of the rarity at some later date.

EARLY COLONIALS

Two of the earliest stamps of New Zealand, of 1855-9, showing Queen Victoria in her coronation robes, after the famous portrait by A. E. Chalon, R.A.

Some of the earliest Colonial overprints, issued in 1881, owing to temporary shortage of stamps. The ½d. and 1d. provisionals were produced by dividing 6d. stamps in half.

The first Australian stamps were of New South Wales and Victoria, issued in 1850. The pictures show the famous and rare "Sydney Views" of New South Wales.

One of the first issues of British Guiana of 1850. Looking like a postmark rather than a stamp, it was type-set in a newspaper printing works. This is the 8 cents green.

A MODERN ERROR

A stamp with an inverted centre: 5 c. of Canada, 1960, issued to commemorate the opening of the St. Lawrence Seaway.

A FAMOUS FORGERY

Two specimens of the "Stock Exchange" forgery of the 1s. stamp of Great Britain of 1867-71.

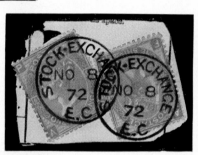

A "TÊTE BÊCHE"

Caused by inadvertently placing one of the dies upside down during the printing process.

VALUE OMITTED

In a pane of 60 stamps of the 1d. of Trinidad, issued in 1901-6, the value to be printed in black was omitted, thus producing a rare variety.

CHAPTER 9

Specialised Collecting

It was once said that " a general collector collects something of everything, a specialist collects everything of something." There is some truth in this, because a collector who decides today to amass stamps from every country of the world can never hope to assemble an even remotely complete collection of any country. On the other hand, a collector focusing his attention upon stamps of, let's say, Australia, can hope to compile an interesting and complete collection of that country. He will be able to include all the different watermarks, perforations, many shades and varieties, adding also, perhaps, a number of entires, special cancellations, First Day letters and such like, without being a rich man.

The British pioneer of philately, Fred. J. Melville, hit the nail on the head when he proclaimed: " The general collector knows less and less about more and more, the specialist knows more and more about less and less." This was said some thirty years ago, when far fewer new issues appeared every year.

While general collecting is an excellent training ground for the beginner, he will fairly soon have to decide on some sort of specialisation if he wants to climb the ladder of philately, by becoming first a " medium collector," and then an " advanced collector."

There is no short cut to specialisation. It would be both boring and foolish to start as a " specialist." Of course, one can decide to collect the stamps of Zululand only. There are 30 stamps of Zululand listed in the Stanley Gibbons catalogue and a small number of varieties.

With an outlay of perhaps £200 a collector could acquire even some of the rare specimens such as the high pound values. The issue of stamps for that colony ceased in 1897 and there will probably never be Zululand stamps again. Thus it would be possible to build up a fairly specialised and complete collection of Zululand.

But in doing this the collector would have to forego most of the joy and excitement philately offers. He would never know anything about the beauty and the intricacies of tens of thousands of stamps of other countries and, indeed, he would never become a real philatelist, though he might have become a " specialist " of Zululand.

As with most things in life a happy compromise is the best solution. General collecting of the stamps of the world is impossible today if the collector desires ever to become more than a hoarder of stamps. Once upon a time one could boast of being the owner of a " good collection of 5,000 stamps." But with more than that number of new stamps appearing annually, from Albania to Zanzibar, from Argentine to Yugoslavia, from Aden to Venezuela, even the keenest amateur would soon turn away in despair from philately, were he to attempt to acquire not only all the stamps issued during a century but also to add every new stamp issued week by week. Not even the richest man in the world, and with all the leisure at his disposal, could ever hope to amass a general collection of such proportions.

Hence, right from the early stages of collecting, the beginner will be well advised to choose a group of countries or a continent as his main interest.

The word " specialisation " is often loosely used. A collector says " I specialise in the stamps of Europe," but what he means is that he collects only stamps of European countries. He is not a specialist at all, but a general collector of Europe.

Collecting Europe, he may subsequently discover that the issues of Denmark or France attract his particular interest. While continuing to collect the other European countries in a general way, he may then begin to concentrate on the two countries. By and by he will become a " specialist " of Denmark and France, or more likely of one of the two countries.

Only persons with a methodical mind and determination to master the many intricacies of philately should embark upon specialisation. To specialise means not only to accumulate as complete a collection of the chosen country and as many of its varieties as possible, but to devote a lot of time and effort to the study of its stamps.

It means that the postal history, perhaps also the political history and the geography and topography of that country, will have to be studied. The postal services prior to the issue of adhesive stamps will be inquired into; the specialist will get in touch with experts and philatelists living in that country; he will read many handbooks and most of them will be available only in the language of that country and require translation. He will subscribe to one or two philatelic journals published in that country, because detailed information will not be readily available from British publications and catalogues.

In the course of his study of, in our case, the stamps of Denmark or France, he will contact postal authorities in Copenhagen or Paris, will attempt to establish friendly relations with Danish or French collectors and will apply for membership of Danish or French philatelic societies. The technicalities of the production of the Danish or French stamps, particularly of the early issues, will have to be studied with the use of official documents, either in the original or a translation.

A specialised collection does not consist merely of stamps. I remember once inspecting a specialised collection of the Ionian Islands, belonging to a distinguished British philatelist. How many people know where the Ionian Islands are situated? I had, myself, only a vague idea. From my school days I recalled that Homer sang about them in the Odyssey and I knew that Ithaca and Corfu were two of them, but I did not remember the names of the four other islands—Paxo, Levkas, Cephalonia and Zante. I knew that Corfu and some of the islands, after a checkered history, became a British protectorate after Napoleon's downfall, and that they remained under British suzerainty until the 1860's when they were reunited with Greece.

A glance through the catalogue provided some philatelic information: from exactly seven lines I learned that three stamps were issued by the British postal authorities in Corfu; the design showed a portrait of Queen Victoria, the stamps were printed in recess by Messrs. Perkins Bacon & Co. in London, appeared on May 15th, 1859, and were ½d. orange, 1d. blue and 2d. carmine. In a footnote in the catalogue it was said that on the 30th May, 1864, the islands were ceded to Greece, when these stamps became obsolete. Then the catalogue editors added: " Collectors are warned to exercise special care in purchasing used specimens as dangerous forgeries have been made with genuine stamps purporting to have been used on original covers."

That was all, and I must confess I felt no desire to become a specialist of the Ionian Islands. Yet my friend proudly produced four large albums. There were pages and pages of Ionian stamps. True, on some pages there was only one or perhaps two stamps, or a rare entire. But even so, my friend had accumulated during more than 30 years of determined search and study a collection of several hundred copies of each of the three values, including a number of rare varieties, shades and entires. There were scores of mint specimens (which, incidentally, are less rare) and many used copies, with postmarks of remote villages. Every page was beautifully written up, with maps showing the islands and the villages from which the particular entire or stamp had come. Several rare printer's proofs were displayed and a few scores of forgeries, each described in detail. Moreover, my friend had been involved in a long correspondence with Messrs. Perkins Bacon & Co., who kindly searched their business archives and obliged him with copies of official documents and letters dating back to the 1850's, concerning the negotiations, specifications and the final order to print the issue. Many other documents, some in fragile, original versions, were included and attractively mounted and framed.

Well, that was a unique case of a specialist of three stamps! To produce such a specialised collection of any other country would be impossible, for the simple reason that no one could acquire such a wealth of documentation about thousands of stamps and varieties issued, for instance, by Denmark or France.

The aim of every specialist is to assemble a philatelic record of " his " country, as searching and complete as possible.

With many specialised collections of the more " popular " countries already in existence, it is today practically impossible to acquire original postal history documents, and quite difficult to assemble a comprehensive show of proofs, essays and rare varieties. However, the budding specialist may be satisfied to embark on specialisation for the sake of study and may be content to pursue it on much more modest lines than my friend of the Ionian Islands.

Some basic rules of specialisation must, however, be observed. A specialised collection should include at least some specimens relating to postal history, such as pre-stamp entires. The designs of every issue should be illustrated in some detail, either by inclusion of artists' essays, or at least by facsimiles or photographs. Catalogues of famous auctions may come in useful here. They contain colour tables of rarities and the appropriate pictures can be cut out and mounted on the margins of the album pages.

Each issue should be properly written up, with the names of the designer, engraver, printer, etc. The correct date when the stamp or stamps first appeared should be stated and details of production, including watermark, perforation, etc. added.

The mounting of the stamps will greatly differ from that of a general collection. I am the happy owner of, among others, a specialised collection of Switzerland. It is housed at the time of writing these lines in twenty-six albums. One album contains, for instance, only the issue of 1862, Sitting Helvetia perforated, and there are several pages reserved for each of the nine values of this issue. As I have several hundred copies and a number of entires of the 2 centimes grey, these specimens are divided in accordance with the classification in the Switzerland Special Catalogue (published by Zumstein & Co., Berne) into the various shades, from light grey to yellow grey, grey, dove grey, silver grey, dark grey and so on. A page contains a few examples of the double print variety of 1878, several other pages display varieties of the 2 centimes stamp, followed by pages with entires, either with the 2 centimes used singly (for printed matter and newspapers) or in combination with other values of this issue, on envelopes, wrappers, money orders, etc. Each page contains some details about the stamps displayed; varieties and plate flaws are illustrated by enlarged drawings and photographs.

I have been specialising in Switzerland for over thirty-five years and as I lived and worked there for some years before the last war I was able to acquire much interesting material for the documentation. My albums containing the modern issues, such as the Swiss charity stamps *Pro Juventute*, are also illustrated with pictures and photographs of the actual scenery, of national costumes, flowers and animals which appear on the designs of the stamps. All relevant data is mentioned in the writing-up of each page.

Specialisation requires not only assiduous research but also the acumen of finding the coveted items. A specialist may buy a large packet of stamps of " his " country (the so called " kilo packets " are sold by weight) and then spend many evenings looking through thousands of quite common stamps until his patience is rewarded by the discovery of, perhaps, just one minor variety or a few interesting cancellations.

A Great Britain specialist I know accumulated more than 300,000 copies of the 1d. red. But he maintains that he still does not possess all existing plates, varieties of engraving and of blued and ordinary paper, and so on, although he has reconstructed many sheets according to plates and corner letters.

Specialising in a country never comes to an end: there is always something to discover and add. Even if everything worthwhile has been assembled regarding printing, paper, watermark, perforation and gum, there is still the wide field of postmarks open to the specialist's research. He will study forgeries, fakes, reprints, essays, proofs, colour trials, and there will always be something to learn and to discover.

If all this sounds rather overwhelming to the beginner, I must remind him that there are many philatelic books published about groups of countries and single countries, from which information can be culled.

As with any other aspect of the hobby, specialisation can

be tackled according to one's particular interest and with due regard to one's financial means. If you decide that specialising in a country from the first to the latest issue would be impossible because the early issues are now in the rarity class and far too expensive to acquire, then there is always a possibility of starting to specialise, let's say, from 1900 or even 1945 onwards. Quite a few specialists do this and I have seen wonderfully arranged collections which gained awards in international exhibitions, containing only modern stamps, but proving that their owners had made a thorough study of the limited subject, without spending a great amount of money on classic rarities.

A word about " specialities " should be added, for those who do not quite understand what philatelic specialisation means. Somebody who collects only First Day covers, or stamps showing designs of animals or ships, is not a specialist. He will have to be satisfied to be a " thematic collector " and his particular sideline of philately is described in Chapter 11.

Neither is someone who sticks stamps on a lampshade or a waste paper basket a philatelic specialist. Household articles thus adorned may look quite attractive but are abhorred by serious philatelists.

CHAPTER 10

Aero-philately

The tremendous development of aviation not only revolutionised the postal services but also opened a new field to stamp collectors—aero-philately.

Airmail collecting has, indeed, become a hobby within a hobby and there are many collectors who specialise exclusively in this sideline. They collect not only airmail stamps but flown letters, pioneer flights mail, first day letters sent by airmail on the occasions of the opening of new air routes, balloon post items, airgraphs and aerograms. Airmail philatelists are also ardent students of many matters connected with aviation and its exciting history.

Many airmail collectors have assembled fine collections showing aircraft types in peace and war and portraits of famous aviators who have been honoured by commemorative stamps. It may, therefore, be fitting to recall in this chapter some of the landmarks in the development of aviation and airmail.

The conveyance of letters by air is, of course, much older than the invention of the aeroplane. If we disregard carrier pigeons which were used for sending messages from time immemorial, we might date the beginning of airmail from the " post balloons " sent out from besieged Paris in 1870.

When the Prussian and Bavarian armies defeated Emperor Napoleon III at Sedan and smashed their way to the gates of the French capital, Paris was completely cut off from all communication with the outside world. For some weeks carrier pigeons were used, but most of them found their way into the boiling pots of the starving population inside and outside the city.

It was an Englishman, Mr. Gibson Bowles, who had the idea of using balloons for carrying mail out of Paris. He was one of the many English newspaper correspondents who had gone to France to report the Franco-Prussian war and he was trapped in the beleaguered capital. Anxious to communicate with his newspaper in London, the *Daily News*, he submitted his plan to the Postmaster General of the provisional government of the Third Republic. At first his idea was regarded as " utterly fantastic," but the government soon had second thoughts about it.

On September 23rd, 1870, the first balloon was released, piloted by the aeronaut Durouf, who volunteered to run the risk of being shot down by one of the many shells of the Prussian artillery. He took off at 8 a.m. and landed three hours later at Craconville, in the department of Eure, with two sacks of letters and official messages, weighing nearly 250 lbs. The area where he landed was not occupied by the enemy, and the messages were the first to reach the outside world from Paris. Soon a regular postal service *Par Ballon Monté* was organised.

Many balloons were destroyed or shot down by the Prussians soon after the take off, and only a few were manned. But some made astonishingly long and successful journeys. Three landed in Belgium, several sailed to Holland, and a few even crossed the Channel. The balloon *Le Jacquard* left Paris on November 28th, 1870 with nearly 500 lbs. of mail. It was lost at sea off the Cornish coast and the pilot, M. Prince, was drowned, but English fishermen salvaged one sack of letters near Falmouth. The balloon letters bore postage stamps and were cancelled with dated postmarks. They arouse great interest in collectors and for some of these balloon letters very high prices are paid.

Less than twenty years after Lord Tennyson wrote of the " heavens filled with commerce and pilots of the purple twilight dropping down with costly bales . . ." his vision came true. It was on December 17th, 1903, that Orville Wright took off at Kitty Hawk, North Carolina, in the first heavier-than-air machine which ever carried man.

In 1928 the United States Post Office issued two stamps to commemorate the International Civil Aeronautics Conference. On the 2 cents value the first Wright machine is pictured, a strange contraption of canvas and wires.

At the same time as the Wright brothers were conducting their experiments in America, a number of other aviators completed their plans in Europe. The most outstanding was a French engineer, Louis Blériot. One of his machines, Mark XI, with which he had undertaken long flights, is shown on the French airmail stamp, issued in 1934, in celebration of the 25th anniversary of his first crossing of the Channel by air.

On July 25th, 1909 at 4.35 a.m., Blériot took off just outside Calais for his venture that made aviation history. The flight was made after a prize was offered by the *Daily Mail* for the first aeroplane successfully crossing the Channel. Blériot earned the £10,000 in exactly 37 minutes —he landed at 5.12 a.m. in North Fall Meadow near Dover —but it took him years to improve his machine before its construction was sound enough to embark on such an ambitious flight.

Blériot and his monoplane have been featured on a number of other stamps, apart from that of his homeland. Lebanon, Tunis and Monaco honoured him in this way, and an attractive stamp showing his machine was issued in 1932 by Latvia.

A year after Blériot's daring feat, the first post flight was carried out in Britain. On the occasion of the Coronation of King George V, privately printed postcards were issued, bearing the picture of Windsor castle. These postcards could be sent by air from London to Windsor on a special flight arranged by the Aero Club. The G.P.O. co-operated and the cards (for which the postal charge was only the usual one penny) were postmarked with a special cancellation reading "FIRST UNITED KINGDOM AERIAL POST WINDSOR-LONDON."

It was not until 1917 that the first airmail service was established. In that year the Italian Post Office issued the first postage stamp for use on air letters. It served for the experimental air line between Rome and Turin. The stamp was a 25 centesimi value, normally used for Express letters, but specially overprinted for this occasion with the date of the flight and the inscription:

"Posta Aerea—Torino-Roma—Roma-Torino"

This first airmail stamp was followed by another, also issued in 1917, for the seaplane service between Naples and Rome, which was established to evade interruption of mail by submarines during the war. Already in 1913 several unofficial "air labels" were issued in several countries, particularly in Switzerland and France, for experimental flights and aviation meetings.

The first regular air route carrying mail was started in May, 1918, and in this new and decisive development America took the lead. The route operated between Washington, Philadelphia and New York. A special 24 cents stamp, showing an aeroplane of nondescript type, was issued. The service proved so successful that within two months the airmail fee was reduced to 16 cents, and before the end of the year to only 6 cents. Soon afterwards, a number of other regular airmail services were installed in the United States.

The earliest Atlantic flights—long before Lindbergh made his famous " dash across the big water "—took place in 1919. A 3 cents stamp of Newfoundland with the picture of a caribou was used for the brave, but unsuccessful, attempt by H. G. Hawker and K. Mackenzie to carry the first mail from North America to England in May of that year. There were only ninety-six copies of this stamp, overprinted with the inscription " First Trans-Atlantic Air Post," which were recovered on the letters damaged by sea water, when the aircraft crashed in the Atlantic. The aviators, the engine and some of the mail were saved, and the stamps are now among the great treasures of collectors, each worth about £700. In June of the same year, John Alcock and A. Whitten Brown accomplished the air crossing from Newfoundland, and this memorable flight brought a 15 cents stamp with an overprint " Trans-Atlantic Air Post 1919—One Dollar." In 1969 the 50th anniversary of this feat was commemorated with the issue of a British 5d. stamp depicting the two fliers above the fuselage of their aeroplane. (See illustration facing p. 128).

In later years Newfoundland, as the convenient taking-off place for Atlantic flights, provided special stamps for the De Pinedo flight in 1927, the Columbia flight in 1930, the Dornier Do-X flights in 1932 and also issued several airmail stamps for regular routes.

While aviators succeeded in conquering the skies over the Atlantic, on the opposite side of the globe other fliers prepared the first air crossing of the Pacific. Three stamps issued by Australia in 1931 commemorate the amazing achievements of Kingsford-Smith, whose name is linked for ever with the history of aviation. The stamps show the two hemispheres and above them Kingsford-Smith's famous plane, " Southern Cross." A magnifying glass enables us to read the name and the registration letters VH-USU on the three-engined Fokker machine, which was flown by Sir Charles Kingsford-Smith right round the world—across the Equator, across the Pacific, across Australia, across the Atlantic, and across the American continent!

Kingsford-Smith used his aircraft for many of his subsequent great flights, and in 1929 he flew the " Southern Cross " from Australia to England. The Australian stamps commemorating his achievements are interesting mementoes, but many collectors treasure the covers of letters carried by Kingsford-Smith on his many mail-carrying flights. Among them are the " experimental mail flights " from Britain to Australia arranged by the Imperial Airways (now B.O.A.C.). These flights opened a new era of Commonwealth communications.

In 1930 Spain issued an interesting series of airmail stamps commemorating the Spanish Latin American Exhibition held in Seville. Some famous aviators and their machines are featured on these stamps; the 10 centavos and 25 centavos values depict the Argentine airman T. Fels and the Chilean pilot, Godoy, who crossed the Andes by air, while on the 50 centavos value the Portuguese, Cabral and Coutinho are honoured for their South Atlantic flight in 1922. Colonel Lindbergh is portrayed on the 1 peseta stamp of this series. Although no British aviator figures in this series, many of the aeroplanes depicted were British made. The 50c. stamp gives an excellent picture of the British Fairey Aviation seaplane, built in 1921 for the Portuguese Government, which Captain Saccadura Cabral and Captain Gago Coutinho used in their trans-atlantic flight.

Another British machine, a standard Fairey 3D seaplane, was taken to Fernando Naronha by a Portuguese warship and flown to St. Paul's Rock where Cabral and Coutinho took it over and reached Brazil. Portugal issued a long set of airmail stamps in 1923, in honour of these two airmen. The design incorporated their portraits and a picture of the Fairey seaplane in which they completed the flight.

Most countries have honoured their pioneers of aviation

110

on stamps. On French stamps we see Clement Ader, the designer of one of the earliest flying machines of modern times, and famous aviators, such as Jean Mermoz, Saint Exupéry and Dagnaux; later several sets of French airmail stamps were issued, showing aircraft over Paris, Marseilles, Lille and other French cities.

The Soviet Union has issued more airmail stamps than any other country. The first Russian stamp depicting an aircraft appeared as early as 1922, and later hardly a year passed without stamps dedicated to propaganda for military and civil aviation. A special feature of the Soviet airmail stamps are the pictures of balloons and airships which appeared on stamps in 1931, 1934, and 1938. In 1945, on nine stamps, Russia depicted some of her Red Air Force machines in dramatic air combats with the German Luftwaffe. Hitler, too, made great use of German stamps for propaganda, before and during the war. Pictures included the Zeppelin, paratroops jumping from aircraft, and even the rockets which the Führer was sending to bomb England.

But in most other countries the pictures of aeroplanes on stamps were used as symbols of the peaceful conquest of the skies. They bear witness to the amazing development of the aeroplane during the last three decades and the expansion of airmail services. This progress is well illustrated on a set of three stamps of India, issued in February, 1961, one of which depicts the giant Boeing 707 jet-airliner together with the Humber-Sommer biplane of 1911. The first successful flight of the Concorde in March 1969 was celebrated by the issue of special stamps both in Great Britain and France. (See illustraion facing p. 128.)

There are now many stamp dealers who specialise in airmail stamps, flown letters and other aero-philatelic items, and several airmail catalogues are published regularly.

A modest side-line of aero-philately is the collecting of

labels issued by post offices to indicate that the letter shall be carried by airmail. Most of us are familiar with the small blue labels with the incription "BY AIR—PAR AVION," but there are many interesting foreign labels, some showing pictures of aircraft. Most of the labels have the inscription in two languages, that of the issuing country and French, which is the international language of the Universal Postal Union.

Airmail stamps are normally collected in the same way as any other stamps, namely in albums, but many collectors take pride in accomplishing some particularly elaborate "writing-up," giving details about the aircraft type shown on the stamps, adding a brief history of the first flight, the biographies of portrayed aviators, and so on. One can see at international exhibitions superb airmail collections including many documents, route maps, drawings of the aeroplanes, pictures or photographs of airports and even highly technical illustrations of the engines.

Flown letters and interesting flight covers and postcards are best collected in transparent envelopes which can be hinged to album pages so that the reverse side can also be inspected. Most flown letters bear arrival or other postmarks on the reverse and wartime airmail covers often have censorship or military marks of historical interest.

A new field of aero-philately was created by the launching of rockets into outer space. Since 1957 the Soviet Union and many other countries issued stamps commemorating space flights and depicting astronauts. In 1969, on the occasion of the Apollo space flight, the United States issued a stamp showing "The First Man on the Moon," and other countries followed suit. No doubt, aero-philatelists will soon be able to add to their collections first-day covers posted on the Moon, Mars or Venus.

CHAPTER 11

Thematic Collecting

A thematic stamp collection is one in which the collector confines himself to assembling stamps associated with a particular theme, subject, motive or topic. In Britain this sideline of philately is usually called " thematic collecting," or sometimes " subject philately"; Americans describe it as " topical philately " or " motif collecting." Somewhat sarcastically it has also been called " the poor man's specialising," and this for a good reason, because a thematic collection can be compiled at a very modest outlay.

One of the many attractions of the hobby is that it leaves a practically unlimited choice to the collector to follow his personal interest or fancy. A lover of animals, someone interested in sport, or music, or architecture will find it easy to collect stamps depicting the subject of his particular bent.

One can amass a wonderful zoological or botanical collection, fill many album pages with stamps depicting religious motives, assemble a picture gallery of famous men and women, and subdivide this theme by collecting stamps portraying only statesmen, soldiers, musicians, writers, painters, inventors, explorers or astronauts.

With the multitude of pictorial stamps issued and, undoubtedly, still to come, there is no limit to initiating still more new themes. There are thematic collectors who have produced extremely interesting collections of stamps showing only waterfalls, or mountains, or rivers, while others combine landscape and scenery into one collection.

It may be expected that someone who had seen service in the Royal Navy or the Mercantile Marine, or just loves the sea, might select " Ships and Boats on Stamps " for a subject collection. Equally, a railway enthusiast will find stamps galore depicting railway trains, locomotives, stations and tracks to build up a " Railway" collection. A lover of music or a professional musician is likely to collect stamps showing portraits of famous musicians and add stamps with pictures of musical instruments.

At club displays and stamp exhibitions one can sometimes detect quite surprising ideas of subject philately. For instance, it was a pleasant thought to collect stamps showing " the good things in life," whether (as in one case I have seen) they are represented by stamps depicting beautiful women, wine, beer, tobacco and cigars, or in a more refined way, stamp pictures of jewels, dress fashions, perfumes, or masterpieces of art, whether paintings, sculptures or products of the goldsmith's and silversmith's craft.

The newcomer to thematic collecting will rightly ask: " But are there enough stamps showing, for instance, sculptures, to compile even a small but worthwhile collection on this subject? " The answer is that, with hardly any exception, every subject can be found on stamps. Many postal authorities, having realised the interest of a great number of collectors in " subjects," have been extremely obliging in providing some stamps with most extraordinary designs.

Obviously the motive which prompts postal authorities to do this is a selfish one. Many small countries derive a large revenue from the sale of stamps to collectors. Having realised that pictorial stamps find ready sales, some postal authorities have made a big business out of issuing stamps that will attract still more buyers.

As a prominent British " scientific philatelist," rightly

disturbed about the flood of pictorial stamps, put it: "They want stamps—they shall have stamps! And the stamp printing presses of Europe, Asia, Africa, America and Australia began pouring out countless specimens of fruit, flowers, ships, railway engines, animals, insects and the like."

Publicity managers and public relations experts in industry and commerce have quickly taken heed of the advertisement value of such pictorial stamps for their particular merchandise or trade.

A petrol company provided an "Oil Stamp Album," listing, describing and illustrating hundreds of stamps from many different countries (from Austria and Azerbaidjan to Rumania, Trinidad and Venezuela) showing prospecting for oil, oilfields, derricks, oil refineries, tankers, petrol tanks, pump stations, oilheating plants and so on, thus encouraging the collecting of " oil stamps " as a means of advertising. Another pamphlet advocates the collecting of " tobacco stamps " and its publishers obviously regard it as good publicity for their industry.

Often stamps with a special subject are issued to boost the national prestige or the export industry of a country. Several South American states produce stamps showing coffee—from the growing plant to the finished product packed ready for shipment. Cuba, Bulgaria and some other countries depict on their stamps tobacco and cigars, and France issues stamps showing Parisian fashion models, cosmetics and perfumes. Recent British series have featured the countryside, cathedrals, inventions and various technical achievements of British industry and the British post office.

It is, however, not always by such obvious publicity that a thematic collector can assemble an out-of-the-ordinary thematic album. A friend of mine whose business is in the "licensed trade," decided to start an appropriate subject collection and, having assembled the most obvious examples, began a lengthy and laborious scrutiny of every stamp illustrated or described in any catalogue, in order to find a bottle, a tankard or a glass, full or empty, on a stamp design. He found quite a few instances on some most unlikely stamps, such as one issued by Egypt commemorating the signing of the Anglo-Egyptian Treaty in 1936—incidentally the only stamp depicting Sir Anthony Eden (now Lord Avon), who represented Britain at the conference. This stamp shows the delegates sitting at a long conference table on which several carafes and glasses can be seen. Although these vessels certainly did not contain any intoxicating liquor but probably only water to refresh the throats of the speakers, my friend decided that it was a good enough example to include in his collection.

Thus one can see that the thematic collector will have to examine many stamps—some issued a long time ago—which include in their designs a connection (however remote) with his "theme." While there are now several thousand stamps showing animals, many of them produced deliberately for the "zoo collector," it is sometimes by pure chance that a stamp designer has put a tiny bird into the sky over the picture of a seascape. The zoo collector will discover with delight that on a 50c. stamp of El Salvador issued in 1924, showing Christopher Columbus and his captains, there is a sleeping dog under the table, and that in the frame surrounding the portrait of King George VI on the 2c. Centenary stamp of Hong Kong of 1941 there are four tiny bats.

As always in philately, the collector has to use his eyes. While a collector of animal stamps can buy complete sets depicting wild beasts, birds, fishes, or insects, he will derive much more satisfaction from discovering for himself the picture of a tiny fish hidden, perhaps, in the frame or the background of some ordinary stamp not deliberately produced for him.

Sports enthusiasts have a very wide field indeed from which to gather specimens for a thematic collection. Quite apart from the many stamps issued on the occasion of the Olympic Games, there are many hundreds more depicting every aspect of outdoor recreation and games, as well as indoor sports. A short alphabetical list of sports and games on stamps includes: angling, archery, baseball, basketball, boating, bob-sleighing, boxing, cycling, diving, fencing, football, gliding, golf, gymnastics, high jumping, hiking and rambling, horse racing, horsemanship, hunting, hurdling, hurley, judo, lawn tennis, motor cycling, motoring, parachute jumping, putting the shot, rugby football, running, scouting, sculling, sea shore games, shooting, show jumping, skating, ski-ing, steeplechasing, swimming, table tennis, throwing the discus, hammer, javelin, tug-of-war, walking, wrestling and yachting. Until recently there had been no trace of cricket on stamps. But this omission was fully rectified when in 1968 Guyana and Jamaica issued three stamps on the occasion of the M.C.C. West Indies Tour. In August 1969 Grenada followed with four even more attractive stamps, depicting batsmen playing various attacking and defensive strokes.

It is, of course, impossible within this small volume to take more than a brief glance at thematic collecting. It must be left to the collector to exercise his own imagination when embarking on this sideline of philately. But, as with stamp collecting in general, there has been in recent years a development in thematic collecting towards a more methodical, one might almost say " scientific", treatment and presentation.

It may satisfy some collectors to accumulate many hundreds of stamps showing pictures of animals or flowers. But the next step is to classify these pictures, Here the collector cannot expect much help from the stamp catalogue, although some of the large catalogues give a brief description or even include the zoological or botanical name of an animal or a plant. As a rule, the collector will have to turn to a natural history book or a handbook on botany, borrowed from a public library.

If he is already a keen naturalist he will have little difficulty in describing the "subject" on most of the stamps. He will divide the stamps according to their zoological designs, that is, mount the apes and monkeys on one or two pages, follow with the carnivorous mammals, such as cats (separating again the lions, tigers, panthers, pumas and so on), the whales, the bats and rodents, fill many pages with the huge family of cattle and ruminants, from the buffalo on a stamp of the United States to the many antelopes and springboks of African stamps. He will arrange his collection into the classes prescribed by zoology, namely mammals, birds, reptiles, amphibia, fishes, insects and spiders, crustacea, and down to the invertebrata, the worms and snails, jelly-fishes and sea-anemones, all of which can be found pictured on stamps.

He will write up his "zoo collection," giving the names of the classes, families and tribes; perhaps also include some drawings or photographs. Thus his "stamp zoo" will enhance not only his own interest in natural history but certainly also attract the attention of his family members and friends who might not be interested in stamps and stamp collecting, but will admire such a fine show of pictures from the animal kingdom.

I have described a "zoo collection," but the same applies to any other thematic collection, which should be thoughtfully assembled, attractively mounted and carefully written up.

If the subject is "Ships on Stamps," then the collector will separate the designs showing native canoes, rowing boats, yachts, sailing ships, great liners and men-of-war and he will find a large number of stamps of many countries showing ship designs. Then, he might do well to include, on separate pages, the stamps with the pictures of famous navigators and seamen, such as Columbus, Vasco da Gama, John Cabot, Sir Humphrey Gilbert, Captain Cook, Nelson and Sir Francis Chichester and his boat.

Again, if the collector's interest is literature or painting, there is a multitude of stamps to produce a fine show. Strangely enough, a stamp showing our national poet, Shakespeare, was first issued in Hungary, long before the 1964 " Shakespeare Festival " British stamp set. The 1948 Hungarian set featured not only Shakespeare but also Mark Twain, Edgar Allan Poe, Goethe, Victor Hugo and Byron. Byron's portrait appeared also on two Greek stamps, issued in 1924, to commemorate the centenary of the Battle of Missolonghi during the Greek War of Independence in which Lord Byron took part.

For the portrait of another giant of English literature, Bernard Shaw, one has to look among the stamps of the Soviet Union which issued a stamp after his death, celebrating him as one of the great Socialist writers. Robert Louis Stevenson appeared on a British Commonwealth stamp, a 7 pence value of Western Samoa the scene of *Treasure Island*, in 1939.

Most postal authorities have made a point of commemorating the famous sons of their countries on special stamps. France, Austria, Italy, Germany, the United States, the Soviet Union and the Communist satellite states, in particular, have issued a very large number of stamps with portraits of poets and writers such as Virgil, Dante, Voltaire, Molière, Racine, Baudelaire, Rabelais, Balzac, Victor Hugo, Anatole France, Stendhal, Flaubert, Jules Verne, Goethe, Schiller, Walt Whitman, Tolstoy, Gorky, Chekhov; of great inventors, scientists and explorers, such as Galileo, Galvani, Volta, Ampère, Fulton, Franklin,

Morse, Edison, Marconi, Pasteur and Madam Curie, not forgetting Charles Darwin whose portrait appears on a stamp of Ecuador which he visited in 1836, and George Stephenson, the inventor of the locomotive, who is commemorated on a Hungarian stamp. Britain, too, has in recent years begun to issue such stamps and they commemorate Sir Winston Churchill, Joseph Lister, Robert Burns and Mrs. Pankhurst. The 1s. 6d. stamp issued in August 1969 to mark the centenary year of the birth of Mahatma Gandhi was the first British stamp ever to portray a foreign celebrity.

Practically all the great painters and sculptors appear on stamps of their own countries. The long list includes Leonardo da Vinci, Michelangelo, Rembrandt, Rubens, Dürer, Holbein, Goya, Van Gogh, Renoir, Cézanne and Rodin. Many of their masterpieces are also represented on stamps, such as da Vinci's " Mona Lisa," several works of the Dutch masters, and Goya's " La Maja." British special issues have in recent years depicted paintings by Sir Thomas Lawrence, John Constable, George Stubbs, and by two contemporary artists, L. S. Lowry and John Piper. There are also a few examples of modern " abstract " art, for instance on an Italian stamp issued on the occasion of an exhibition in Milan in July, 1951.

A good example of how a fascinating thematic collection on " Music " can be assembled is the famous collection of the late Mr. Theodore Steinway, head of the piano manufacturing firm of world repute. From the vast reservoir of stamps portraying famous composers, Mr. Steinway could, of course, easily accumulate a portrait gallery that included Beethoven, Mozart, Haydn, Handel, Schubert, Bach, Wagner, Brahms, Johann Strauss (all of whom appeared on stamps of Austria and Germany, which also issued stamps portraying Richard Strauss, Wilhelm Furtwängler and other musicians of more recent times), Berlioz, Debussy, Gounod, Saint-Saëns (on French stamps), Bellini, Rossini, Donizetti, Corelli, Verdi, Puccini and others (on Italian stamps), many famous Russian composers, Chopin on a Polish stamp, Liszt, Goldmark, and such " moderns " as Bartok and Kodály on Hungarian stamps.

But Mr. Steinway went much further. Richard Wagner's work was illustrated by several German stamps depicting the " Nibelungen " from which the composer took his theme for the " Ring," the Bellini set issued by Italy provided a stamp showing Bellini's house and another his piano. When a Polish stamp appeared with the portrait of the famous pianist, Paderewski, Mr. Steinway received from him an autographed copy. There are many stamps showing musical instruments, from the harp on Irish issues to native tom-tom drums on a number of African colonial stamps, and also an Italian stamp with the famous violin-maker, Stradivarius. The collection was soon extended into a display of every instrument depicted on stamps. These included even posthorns, as well as military trumpets which Mr. Steinway noticed on war stamps showing marching soldiers. His collection grew into three tightly packed volumes and gained high awards at many international exhibitions. It became a potted " History of Music " on stamps.

The thematic collector will be well advised to keep the historical interest in mind when planning a collection on any subject. Most pictorial stamps are issued to celebrate or commemorate some special occasion or anniversary and thus already stress the historical angle.

Doctors, many of whom are keen philatelists, have assembled subject collections on medicine, and one I have seen on the " History of Medicine on Stamps " includes not only stamps portraying famous physicians, biologists and surgeons, but also stamps showing hospital buildings, surgical instruments, X-ray apparatus and a great number of doctors and nurses at work. Then there are things connected with the Red Cross (up to now more than 700 stamps have been issued either to celebrate Red Cross anniversaries, or in aid of its funds) which can be included in this "Medicine" collection. Stamps portraying Aesculapius, the Greek god of medicine, or his familiar staff with the serpent curling around it, as well as Aesculapius's daughter, Hygeia, goddess of health (who gave the name to hygiene) were added.

One of the most fascinating subjects is "Religion on Stamps." Here the collector can find stamps galore illustrating any religion, from idol worship of primitive races (on many colonial stamps) to Judaism (on the stamps of Israel), Islam, Buddhism and Christianity. Cardinal Spellman, the Roman Catholic Archbishop of New York and a prominent philatelist, assembled a unique collection on this subject which won gold medals at many international exhibitions.

There are several thousand stamps which could supply not one but several different thematic collections on Christian religion. The story of Christ's life can be illustrated by stamps, as can the lives of many saints. There is a multitude of stamps showing famous cathedrals and churches all the world over. Here I can give but a few examples of the "British section." On the 1899 and 1920 issues of Malta we find St. Paul preaching after his ship-wreck and the attack by the asp. St. Paul appears again on the 10s. value of 1938, side by side with a portrait of King George VI., and in 1960 a whole series was issued commemorating the 19th centenary of the shipwreck of St. Paul. In the litany of saints on British colonial stamps we find St. Publius, with St. Paul and alone, on Maltese stamps; St. Barnabas on those of Cyprus (several of which also depict the Cathedral of St. Nicholas at Famagusta and the Church of St. John at Kalopanayotis); St. Ursula on stamps of the Virgin Islands; St. Helena on those of the island named after her; and St. George on many Commonwealth stamps and several of Great Britain.

Stamps of the Vatican State bear, almost without exception, religious themes, while anyone deciding to make up a thematic collection dealing exclusively with the Reformation, and Protestant denominations, will find stamps portraying Martin Luther, Calvin, Zwingli, John Knox and a large number of Protestant churches and chapels. The Salvation Army, too, has been portrayed on stamps in a 1965 British set commemorating the Army's centenary.

Thematic collections have been built up on geographical (with stamps showing maps and topographical designs), archaeological, anthropological (showing various human races and customs), technological and heraldic subjects. With the advent of space travel, collections are being assembled showing the progress made in the conquest of space by rockets and satellites.

Heraldry is an obvious and easy choice as thousands of stamps of every country depict coats of arms, regalia and other emblems. Retired generals, colonels and admirals have produced some marvellous thematic collections of military subjects showing marching units, cavalry charging, guns blazing, fierce battles fought, warships engaged, and of course, page after page of stamps illustrating splendid uniforms worn by kings, dictators and liberators, victorious generals and conquerors of centuries past.

A thematic collection can mirror the individual interest of its owner, and it will arouse interest in anyone to whom it is shown. It also has the advantage that it is always "complete," because there is no steadfast rule of what to include and what to omit. It can be assembled economically, because the collector can safely decide to exclude some of the expensive stamps, without destroying the fascination and the beauty of the display.

But one must keep in mind that thematic collecting is but a sideline of philately and one which can be pursued only in a lighter vein. It is not a substitute for serious collecting, although it may well provide educational profit and relaxation from the preoccupation with the intricacies of " scientific philately."

CHAPTER 12

Famous Collectors and Collections

With a small but neatly arranged stamp collection of his own, Prince Charles, the Prince of Wales, is expected to continue the philatelic hobby in the fourth generation of the Royal Family. His first collection was presented to him, when he was still a baby, by the schoolchildren of Dartford. They formed a committee, none of whose members was older than ten; teachers were taken into their confidence and the children brought either stamps or sixpences for the Prince's gift. A deputation proceeded to Clarence House (then the home of Princess Elizabeth and the Duke of Edinburgh) to present the collection. When Prince Charles was sent to Cheam School, he might have found the little album a good start to philately, even though he will one day be the owner of one of the greatest and most valuable collections in the world.

This is the Royal Collection formed by his great-grandfather King George V, who was an enthusiastic philatelist all his life. He started the hobby when a naval cadet at Dartmouth. Later, as a midshipman and young officer in the Royal Navy, he brought stamps from his long sea-journeys to many countries of the British Empire, which he was destined to rule for a quarter of a century.

In those early days between 1882 and 1901 he shared the interest in the hobby with many other naval men, such as Admiral Sir W. H. Bruce, Captain Glossop of *H.M.S. Sydney* and Commander Napier, who were at one time his superior officers and themselves distinguished philatelists.

In 1893, the year of his marriage to the Princess Mary of Teck—later Queen Mary—he joined the London

Philatelic Society and was elected its president three years later. The Society's secretary, Mr. J. A. Tilleard, advised the Prince to abandon collecting foreign countries and to concentrate upon British Empire stamps. At the end of the last century the collection of the then Duke of York already contained many valuable items, but consisted of only five or six albums. Twenty years later, when their owner had become King George V, it had grown to some forty stout volumes and the king decided to house them in a special "Stamp Room" at Buckingham Palace. The first Keeper of the "Royal Collection" was Mr. Tilleard. For 30 years Sir John Wilson, Bt., occupied this position and he was succeeded in July 1969 by Mr. J. B. Marriot, a housemaster at Charterhouse public school.

Already in 1896 the Prince, as President of the London Philatelic Society, taking a very personal interest in its activities and attending its meetings and displays, asked his father, King Edward VII, to grant the Society a charter and the prefix "Royal," and he became its patron.

When an international stamp exhibition took place in London in 1923, King George V visited it several times and gave a reception at Buckingham Palace for more than a hundred distinguished collectors from all over the world who had come to London. The King, who by then had been collecting for more than half a century, surprised the experts by his great knowledge of postal history.

His son, King George VI, who inherited the Royal Collection and succeeded his father as the Patron of the Royal Philatelic Society, was not merely continuing a royal tradition. Nor was he only an "amateur." He, too, had collected stamps since boyhood and had assembled a splendid collection of his own. When he inherited his father's famous collection, called the "Red Collection" because of the colour of the leather covers of the albums, he decided to carry on independently with his own collection, which became the " Blue Collection," bound in blue morocco.

While the " Red Collection " already contained many outstanding rarities, some of which King George V had acquired at international auctions and from leading dealers, paying handsome prices from his private purse, the " Blue Collection " became practically unique as regards British Empire and Commonwealth issues. It is not confined to stamps only, but includes practically all the artists' sketches, original drawings, dies and plates, proofs and colour trials of every stamp issued during the reign of its owner. To these all the relevant items have been added during the reign of our present Queen.

All postal authorities of the British Commonwealth submit the final stamp designs for royal approval. It is not merely a matter of form. On several occasions King George VI suggested alterations in the designs, examining them with the eyes of an experienced philatelist. His service as a sailor stood him in good stead when choosing stamp designs. When the Colonial Office and the Crown Agents submitted for the King's approval the designs for the first set of stamps for Pitcairn Island, in 1940, a picture of the armed vessel *Bounty* of Mutiny fame was selected for the 6d. value. The King discovered that in the artist's drawing the ship's sails were wrongly rigged. With a smile, he remarked: " The *Bounty* could not sail in the manner her sails are drawn . . ." and wrote a " NO! " on a little piece of paper, which he attached with a pin to the design. It was duly corrected by the artist and a philatelic error was avoided.

The Royal Collection contains many errors and varieties, apart from many unique pieces. Among these are two blocks of four of the £1 stamp of St. Vincent, issued to commemorate the Royal Silver Wedding in 1948. These stamps were printed in London and the entire consignment was lost at sea when the ship carrying it foundered. The only surviving copies were the eight stamps sent to the King immediately after printing. They were printed in black, and when the £1 value was produced again the colour was changed to purple.

At least once, however, even the King had to buy a British stamp from a dealer. One day a half-crown stamp booklet was sold over a post office counter. Its buyer discovered that the booklet contained two 2½d. stamps printed head to foot in relation to their neighbours. King George VI hearing about the find—which the fortunate buyer had sold to a stamp dealer—was keen to include this exceptional " tête-bêche " in his collection and paid £135 for it.

The " red " and " blue " albums of the " Royal Collection " now number well over four hundred and several are added every year. The Queen, who had been a keen collector during her girlhood, is prevented by her arduous duties from taking a regular interest in her collections, but she does visit the " Stamp Room " on occasions and takes an interest in all new stamp issues within her realm.

In newspaper gossip paragraphs one finds, from time to time, the " Blue Mauritius " described as the " rarest stamp in the world." It is certainly a great rarity, but there are many much rarer stamps in the Royal Collection, apart from several covers with superb pairs and singles of the mint Mauritius Twopenny. For instance, the only known mint block of four of the 1d. Queensland 1860, which King George VI acquired when the famous Ferrari collection was auctioned, or the unique block of five mint Mauritius stamps of 1848, with one of the stamps showing the error " Penoe " instead of Pence. Then there is the only existing unused block of the 4c. British Guiana imperforate. There are several collections of original drawings, proofs and trial of the earliest issues of Jamaica, Barbados, Trinidad and the Australian States, all unique.

AERO-PHILATELY

Comprising airmail stamps, flown covers, covers commemorating first and special flights, also aircraft, rockets, satellites and astronauts. *Top:* British stamp issued in 1969 for the 50th anniversary of the first trans-atlantic flight; an early Douglas mail plane; *second row:* a Soviet fighter aircraft of 1937; Austrian airmail stamp of 1925. *Left:* first manned rocket flight to the Moon in 1969; and the Concorde supersonic jet (1969).

THEMATIC COLLECTING

A very popular sideline of philately is collecting stamps according to their designs. The illustrations show a few of the many subjects which thematic collectors choose: "Ships and Seafaring", "Architecture", "Railways and Transport", "Flowers", "Horses", "Famous Men and Women" (the stamp depicts Robert Louis Stevenson).

The " Red Collection " is estimated to be worth well over £1,000,000, but the " Blue Collection " is priceless, because very many items therein exist only in the one specimen. Although the Royal Collection cannot be inspected, the Queen, following the example of her father and grandfather, has always given permission for many of the greatest rarities to be exhibited at international stamp exhibitions in London and the Commonwealth.

The Royal Family share an interest in philately with many crowned heads. King Gustav Adolf of Sweden, the late King Alfonso XIII of Spain, the former Queen of Italy, the late King Fuad of Egypt and the late King Carol of Rumania were famous and active philatelists.

As already mentioned, President Franklin D. Roosevelt was an ardent collector and so were Lord Birkenhead and Lord Grey, who found relaxation in philately from the cares of their cabinet offices. So were, and are, many statesmen, judges, generals and admirals, lawyers and doctors, industrialists and bankers and quite a number of stage and screen stars.

Looking through the membership lists of the Royal Philatelic Society of London we find the names of many distinguished personalities, such as Sultan Mohammad V, the Nawab of Bahawalpur, owner of one of the most valuable Empire collections, Mr. Justice Anglin, the Duke of Argyll, Sir Frederick Brundrett, formerly chief scientific adviser to the Ministry of Defence, Sir Andrew Clark, Q.C., Sir A. Chester Beatty, former President of the Royal Cancer Hospital, Professor V. W. Dix, the eminent surgeon, Sir John Dodd, a former M.P. and President of the Association of British Chambers of Commerce, H. D. Hicks, Q.C., Sir Denys Lowson, a former Lord Mayor of London, Hon. G. C. Marler, P.C., M.P., Sir James Marshall, Sr. Moniz de Aragao, former Ambassador of Brazil, Marquis du Parc Locmaria, the Belgian

Ambassador, General Napier-Clavering, Viscount Parker, Professor R. J. Reynolds, the eminent radiologist of Charing Cross Hospital, Sir David Roseway, a former Under-Secretary of State at the War Office, Sir Gerald Shepperd, former British Ambassador to Iceland, Major-General Shortt, Professor L. D. Stamp, the eminent geographer, Sir Eric Studd, Bt., governor of the Polytechnic, Lord Swaythling, the banker, Admiral Talbott, Dr. L. F. Thomen, Ambassador of the Dominican Republic, Sir Nicholas Waterhouse, a President of the Institute of Chartered Accountants, John Woollam, M.P.—to mention just a few names of distinguished men from different walks of life.

The educational value of stamp collecting was recognised by men such as Matthew Arnold, Queen Victoria's Inspector of Schools, poet and writer, at one time a master at his father's famous school at Rugby, and by Dr. William James (brother of the novelist Henry James), a prominent American educationalist and philosopher. The late George Robey, the Grand Old Man of the English music hall, assembled during his lifetime a superb collection, particularly of the stamps of Portugal and her colonies.

Some of the great British philatelists have donated their treasures to the nation. Foremost among them was Mr. Thomas Keay Tapling, M.P., who died in 1891 at the age of only 36. Having started collecting as a boy, he had accumulated a collection of more than 100,000 stamps, none issued after 1890, and most of the early rarities in wonderful condition. Among them are a Blue Mauritius unused, several exquisite copies of British Guiana, great rarities from Canada, Ceylon, Newfoundland, and other colonies, as well as rare foreign items, such as the 2c. blue of Hawaii, 1851, often described as the rarest stamp in the world after the 1 cent British Guiana.

The Tapling Collection is now housed in the British Museum in London, where is also the Mosley Collection, assembled by Dr. Edward Mosley of Cape Town and donated by his daughter to the British nation. This collection includes some of the rarest stamps of Cape of Good Hope, including both colour errors of the Woodblocks of 1861 and a specialised collection of the Mafeking Siege stamps, issued by General Baden-Powell.

The King's Library at the British Museum also houses one of the finest collections of airmail stamps in the world, airpost curiosities, first flown letters, etc. including a cover franked with the " Hawker " and the " Martinsyde " Atlantic Air Post stamps of 1919, regarded as the rarest airmail cover in existence. This collection was donated by Mrs. E. Fitzgerald, and another famous lady philatelist, Miss Winifred Penn-Gaskell, bequeathed her famous and highly specialised aero-philatelic collection to the Science Museum in Kensington. Apart from many unique British and Commonwealth items, Miss Penn-Gaskell (at one time President of the Helvetia Philatelic Society in London) accumulated many superb items of Swiss Pioneer air-stamps and also many French aero-philatelic rarities.

A great collection of war stamps, issued mainly during the 1914-18 war, is in the Imperial War Museum (London, S.E.1), where there are also several " thematic collections " relating to World War II, such as " A History of the War on Postage Stamps," prefaced by a collection entitled " The Path towards War," showing stamps of Hitler's Germany and Nazi occupied countries. Another collection has the theme " The War in the Far East " and there are also collections showing " military stamp designs," depicting infantry, cavalry, artillery, tanks, battle scenes, aircraft in action, ships, submarines and rockets.

A fine display of modern Empire and Commonwealth

stamps can be inspected at the Commonwealth Institute in South Kensington, London, S.W.7. More recently a magnificent National Postal Museum has been opened in London. It adjoins the London Chief Post Office in King Edward Street, near St. Paul's underground station, and is only a stone's throw from the site of the old General Post Office where the world's first adhesive postage stamps were put on sale in 1840. The Museum aims to stimulate an interest in British postage stamps and in particular to provide philatelists with information about the earliest adhesive postage stamps in the world. It is open to the public each week-day from 10 a.m. to 4.30 p m. and on Saturdays from 10 a.m. to 4 p.m.; admission is free.

The establishment of the Museum resulted from a proposal made by Reginald M. Phillips of Brighton who, in 1965, presented to the nation his unique collection of 19th century British postage stamps, together with a gift of £50,000 to found the Museum.

The National Postal Museum was first opened in September 1966, but thanks to Mr. Phillips' generosity it was greatly extended during 1968 and its fine galleries now cover some 5,000 square feet. The new, greatly enlarged Museum was opened by the Queen on 19 February 1969.

The "midwife" and Curator of the Museum since its inception has been Mr. Marcus Arman and the G.P.O. has been fortunate, indeed, to find such an experienced, imaginative and dedicated official among its own staff. Within a remarkably short time Mr. Arman has become widely known among philatelists for his expertise and enthusiasm. His lively talks to groups of visitors, as well as the regular programme of films and lectures that he has organised, have been deservedly very popular and in a single year the Museum now attracts some 100,000 visitors, many of them from abroad.

The central feature of the National Postal Museum is the

superb Reginald M. Phillips Collection. Comprising 46 volumes it was assembled over a period of forty years and is quite irreplaceable. It documents the conception, planning and issue of the world's first postage stamps and traces the subsequent manufacturing and design developments in British stamp production during the nineteenth century. The Phillips Collection is housed in the Museum's main gallery, with selected items in open frame display cabinets and the remainder in alphabetically-indexed sliding metal frames which can be withdrawn for inspection from wall cabinets.

A selection from the Phillips Collection was awarded the Grand Prix at the London International Stamp Exhibition in 1960. A short account of the Collection, by F. Marcus Arman, is obtainable from the National Postal Museum (price 5s.).

In addition to the Phillips Collection the Museum also contains the unique and priceless Post Office Collection incorporating a vast array of historical documents of great interest to philatelists and postal historians. These treasures include the original dies for the stamps of 1840, printing plates, and the officially approved final proof sheets, known as the " imprimaturs " or " registration sheets ", for almost every stamp and postage label issued since 1840. This unique collection, from which only selections can be displayed at any one time, represents a complete and comprehensive record of the British postage stamp.

The Museum also houses the Post Office collection of stamps issued by member countries of the Universal Postal Union. This " Berne Collection " is an almost complete record of every stamp issued by every postal administration in the world since 1878, and also contains many earlier stamps and specimens of postal stationery. The whole of this collection is accommodated so as to give " open access " to the visitor.

In addition the Museum displays a series of changing exhibitions, each centred on a selected theme and each lasting for a few months. Items not on display are available for inspection by approved students and historians.

National Postal Museum " Notes ", usually written by the Curator, Mr. Arman, appear regularly in the G.P.O.'s monthly *Philatelic Bulletin* which also gives particulars of new British stamp issues and much else of interest to collectors and those interested in postal history. The Bulletin is obtainable from the Philatelic Bureau, 2-4 Waterloo Place, Edinburgh (price: 7s. 6d. per annum).

Two of the greatest collectors in philatelic history were Baron Phillippe Ferrari de la Renotière and Arthur Hind. Baron Ferrari was born in 1848 and began collecting as a boy, maintaining his enthusiasm until his death in 1917. He accumulated the largest and most valuable collection ever assembled. Some of the stamps, which subsequently became priceless rarities, he had bought for a few shillings.

The Ferrari collection was auctioned in Paris between June, 1921 and November, 1925, at thirty-nine separate sales which attracted prominent collectors and dealers from all over the world. If the collection were offered for sale to-day, experts believe it would fetch £5,000,000.

Among the bidders at the Ferrari auctions was Mr. Arthur Hind, a Yorkshire-born American textile millionaire. When he died in the early thirties, his collection, was auctioned, partly in New York and partly in London. Among his treasures was the 1c. British Guiana of 1856, for which Hind had paid £7,756 at the Ferrari auction in 1921. The Hind auctions took place in 1934 and 1935 and realised well over a quarter of a million pounds, although only a part of the collection was disposed of at that time. The British Guiana stamp was sold by Hind's widow privately for £10,000. Eventually the stamp was acquired by an American dealer for 100,000 dollars.

CHAPTER 13

Strange Stories behind Stamps

Every collector nurses the secret hope of making one day a
" great find," discovering a rarity among his modest
duplicates or finding some stamps of great value among the
old letters and papers in grandfather's battered trunk in
the attic. There is also the evergreen hope that one might
walk one day into the village post office, ask for a few
threepenny stamps and be casually handed a pane which
had escaped perforation. Alas, such dreams rarely come
true.

But from time to time lucky " finds " do happen, which
make the unsuspecting finders rich overnight. In January,
1957, 16-year-old Patricia Jarvis bought, at the post office
at Dartford in Kent, a sheet of 240 twopenny stamps.
When she tried to tear some of them from the sheet, she
noticed that they were not perforated. Although knowing
nothing about stamp collecting, she found it odd and
showed the sheet to a Dartford stamp dealer, who immediately offered her £40. This was a modest price—the
stamps were subsequently valued at £9,600.

In 1947 an old " schoolboy's collection " was bought
privately for a few shillings. Among the few hundred
common stamps, most of them in poor condition, was a
perfect specimen of the 1d. orange red of Mauritius. It
was nearly half a century since the last example of this rare
stamp had been discovered. It was subsequently acquired
by Sir Andrew Clark, Q.C. for £1,200.

An even more spectacular find was made in 1946 at
Dalkeith Palace, seat of the Duke of Buccleuch. The

Duke's secretary, Mr. Martin, looking for some old documents of the present duke's grandfather, who was Lord Privy Seal in the reign of Queen Victoria, found an old writing-set with a quill pen, sealing wax, twenty-one embossed letter seals and 55 Penny Black stamps, singles and pairs. At the bottom of the box was also a sheet of what appeared to be gummed paper. When he turned it up he realised that it was a large pane of 48 Penny Black stamps. The pane was in pristine condition. It had lain there for almost a century. The duke's grandfather had paid exactly eight shillings for it. When it was subsequently auctioned by Mr. H. R. Harmer at his Bond Street sale rooms it was sold for £6,000. Today it would probably fetch many times that amount.

When the Penny Black was issued in May 1840, the British public was reluctant to use the new-fangled " bits of coloured paper " for the prepayment of mail. Sales were very slow and most people insisted on sending their missives unfranked, the payment to be collected from the addressee. In Victorian England it was thought impolite to prepay a letter; it was the custom to tip the servant when he delivered a message by hand and this custom was also applied to the postman though he had to hand over the penny to the post office. Some people took umbrage at receiving a pre-paid letter, because it might have been a reflection on their generosity.

Moreover, many people had the feeling that licking the " cement " on the back of the stamp was unhygienic and might cause sickness. Rowland Hill had the difficult task of persuading the British public to use stamps. Leaflets were distributed explaining how they should be affixed and the public was assured that the " cement " was quite harmless to lick. On the margins of every sheet of the Penny Black appeared the inscription: " Price 1 Penny per Label. Place the Label ABOVE the address and towards the Right-hand side of the Letter. In wetting the Back be careful not to remove the Cement."

The inscription gives a clue to the reason why we stick stamps on the upper right corner of an envelope. This rule was accepted in Britain and is now general throughout the world, but abroad in the past stamps were stuck anywhere on the envelope, often on the left side, or below the address, and even on the reverse side.

The reluctance to use the new " adhesive labels," as the first stamps were called, was even greater in some foreign countries. The Postmaster of Geneva, M. Candolle, visited London in 1839 and watched with interest Rowland Hill's preparations for the issue of the Penny Black. He persuaded the Cantonal authorities of Geneva to issue postage stamps too, but when the " double Geneva " 10 centimes stamp appeared, people just refused to buy it and insisted that the postal charge should be collected on delivery. M. Candolle, in desperation, decided to sell the 10c. stamps at a discount of 20%. He hoped to induce his thrifty compatriots to use stamps if they were to pay only 8 centimes, instead of 10 centimes. This had the result hoped for and the Genevois at last got used to the innovation, but it took until the end of 1844 before stamps were generally used and the discount could be discontinued.

The story of the discovery of the famous " topsy-turvy aircraft " stamp of the United States is also one of a lucky find. Only one sheet of the 24 cents airmail stamp was printed with the centre inverted and thus showed the plane performing a strange feat of aerobatics. An office boy bought this complete sheet for his employer at a Washington post office. The youngster was a stamp collector and realised at once that there was something wrong with the stamps. He borrowed a few dollars from his mother, kept the sheet, and bought another of

" normal " stamps for his boss. Although he sold most of the freak stamps to a dealer for a comparatively modest sum, he kept several copies and later made a small fortune out of his lucky purchase.

The story has an even more amusing tail-piece. As soon as pictures and descriptions of the " inverted " stamp appeared in the press, the U.S. Postmaster General issued a ponderous announcement, saying that " the mistake was greatly regretted " and that " all purchasers of the misprints are invited to return the stamps to the nearest post office, where the misprinted stamps will be redeemed and exchanged for correct stamps of 24 cents value." One can imagine that this invitation remained without response. The " inverted " stamp quickly became a great rarity, and when in 1951 a few copies were offered at an auction in America, they fetched more than £1,000 a piece.

When Prince Oldenbourgh of Russia, a cousin of the last Tsar, escaped to Sweden from St. Petersburg at the time of the Bolshevik revolution, he had sewn into the lining of his coat a number of great rarities from his large collection. His health was so badly impaired by the privations he had suffered during the imprisonment before his flight that he forgot all about it on reaching a safe haven. He wore the suit on and off for several years and finally gave it to another Russian émigré. Years went by until the man presented with the suit, made of excellent cloth, took it to a tailor and asked to have it turned. Only when the tailor went to work on it were the stamps found. Some had become crumpled and damaged during the many years they had been hidden between cloth and lining, but quite a few were still in good condition. Among them were several mint copies of United States 24 cents of 1861 in the rare steel-blue colour, each worth more than £100, as well as several other " classic " stamps of Russia, France and the United States. The tailor gave the stamps to his customer who, unaware of their value, gave them to his young son. For fifteen years they remained undiscovered in the schoolboy's collection until he learned more about philately and realised the value of the tucked-away treasures. The stamps were auctioned in London and brought the son of the poor emigrant a tidy sum.

Many rare stamps have an interesting history, such as the only two remaining large panes of one of the earliest Swiss issues, the 5 centimes Waadt of 1849, now in the Postal Museum in Berne. This stamp is of particular interest to the expert because during its printing by the lithographic process the stone of the 4 centimes stamp was used, with the figure " 4 " redrawn into " 5 " on each of the 100 stamps. This resulted in the new figure being slightly different on each of them.

A famous philatelist and author of several important studies on Swiss stamps, Baron Axel de Reuterskiöld, embarked on the difficult task of reconstructing a complete sheet of a hundred of these rare 5 centimes *Poste Locale* of the Canton Waadt. Over the years he had acquired a large number of copies, but it seemed that he would never accomplish his ambition. Then, by one of those unique coincidences that help to advance philatelic research, Reuterskiöld had a stroke of luck. Holidaying in a village near Lausanne, he made friends with a farmer, who showed him a large pane of 48 of this coveted stamp. The farmer kept the pane between the pages of the family Bible and told him that they had lain untouched in the old book for over half a century. The baron made a generous offer but the farmer flatly refused to sell the stamps for cash. But he told Reuterskiöld that he would exchange them for a pair of farm horses. The Baron jumped at the offer, presented the farmer with a sturdy stallion and a strong mare and got the stamps. Today this pane, split into two blocks of 23 and 25 stamps is in the Swiss Postal

Museum. Its present-day value can hardly be estimated but is certainly in the region of £5,000.

When Lady Naylor-Leyland discovered some years ago in her flat in Bruton Street several envelopes with the 5 cents brown of New Brunswick (a North American colony which later became one of the states of Canada) she did not know that she had found treasure. The stamps were auctioned for £5,360 and would be worth much more today. But what interested the philatelist even more than their value was the strange story connected with their issue a century ago.

In 1860, a Mr. Charles Connell was Postmaster of the Province of New Brunswick. The colony had first issued stamps in 1851 and some years later the Lieutenant-Governor ordered Mr. Connell to prepare a new pictorial set, suggesting that it should include portraits of Queen Victoria and the Prince of Wales (later King Edward VII). Mr. Connell arranged the designs and the printing with the American Bank Note Company in New York. In May, 1860, the attractive set, consisting of six values, was duly delivered. But imagine the amazement of the Queen's Lieutenant-Governor when he discovered on the 5 cents stamp not the portrait of the Queen or the Prince but that of Mr. Charles Connell, looking very distinguished, in a high collar and cravat. The governor could do nothing but tender to the Queen his most humble apologies. The Queen was not amused and ordered that the " Connell stamp " should be withdrawn from circulation and the insolent postmaster sacked. This was done and the offensive stamp was quickly replaced by another 5 cents value, this time with the Queen's image. It is the only case of a postmaster honouring himself on a stamp and has since become a classic rarity.

The Panama Canal would have been built five hundred miles to the north and would probably today be called the

" Nicaragua Canal," were it not for a stamp. When the plan for building the canal was discussed by American and French financiers, there were two groups, one in favour of building it through the isthmus of Panama, another supporting a pathway through Nicaraguan territory. In 1896 Nicaragua even issued special stamps, depicting a map and showing how the canal passing through its territory would have the natural advantage of the San Juan River and the great Lake of Nicaragua. For several years the merits of the rival routes were weighed up by the United States Government and Senate. Then, in 1900, the Nicaraguan post office had the unfortunate idea of issuing a set of stamps depicting the volcano of Momotombo. The volcano was extinct for centuries, but the artist, with mistaken pride, drew it with smoke belching from its crater.

One of the French businessmen who supported the Panama project, Colonel Bunaux-Varille, happened to be a stamp collector. He examined the new stamp and had a brainwave. He bought up a large number of the stamps and sent a copy, nicely mounted on a piece of cardboard, with the inscription: " A Postage Stamp of Nicaragua, showing the activity of the Volcano Momotombo; an official witness of the volcanic danger in Nicaragua," to every United States senator and other influential people concerned with the canal project. This was to discourage the authorities from cutting the canal in Nicaragua.

He fully achieved his purpose. One senator after another stood up at the decisive session of the Canal Committee and, waving the card with the stamp, declared that it would be far too risky and a waste of the American taxpayers' money to build the canal through Nicaragua and expose it to destruction by a volcanic eruption. Some senators had studied the Nicaraguan stamp closely and pointed out that in the foreground of the design it showed " the terrible realism of disaster, with people fleeing on to a pier to escape by ship."

Nicaragua lost the contract for a lease and remained a poor country. The canal was built in Panama, on 120,000 acres of arid land for which the Panamanians were paid a substantial compensation in addition to a high annual lease. What happened to the unfortunate artist and the Nicaraguan officials who approved his design, history does not tell, but it is likely that they fell into disgrace with their countrymen.

There are many cases where stamp artists made amazing and amusing blunders in their designs, though never with such far-reaching results as in the case of the Nicaraguan stamp. I mentioned some in Chapter 8, but the list is a long one. Among design errors is another stamp connected with the Panama Canal. When the United States post office issued, in 1912, a set commemorating the opening of the canal, the artist described his picture on the 2 cents stamp as that of the " Gatun Locks." In fact the design showed the " Pedro Miguel Locks," many miles away. The Postmaster General decided to destroy the whole issue of the 2 cents stamp and replace it with one showing the correct locks. The new stamp appeared in 1913, long after the celebrations were over.

An even worse mistake was made on a stamp of the Philippine Islands in 1932, when the artist described the picture on the 18 cents value as that of the Pagsanjan Falls, a famous sight of the Philippines. In fact, it was a picture of the Vernal Falls in the National Park of California. Here, at least, the artist had the good excuse that a post official had given him a wrong photograph from which to copy his design. The Philippine stamp with the Californian view was, however, never withdrawn.

A similar excuse was tendered by the artist who designed the 5 cents stamp of the United States issue in 1925, commemorating the Vikings landing in America. The ancient ship was depicted flying the Norwegian flag at the stern and the Stars and Stripes at the prow—allegedly in the 9th or 10th century! The explanation was that the artist used a photograph of a " Viking Barque " built in 1890 in Norway, and modelled on an ancient Viking ship unearthed from the mud at Gokstad. This barque manned by a rowing team of twelve sailed to the World Fair in Chicago in 1893 and did display the national flags of Norway and the United States.

We cannot really blame the artists who, for nearly half a century on successive issues of St. Kitts-Nevis, have depicted Christopher Columbus sporting a long telescope. This was a rather silly anachronism because the telescope was not invented until the early 17th century, more than 150 years after Columbus's voyage to America. The artists were, however, merely copying the colony's coat of arms which shows Columbus with the telescope, and the blame must be attached to the heraldic expert who devised this badge during Queen Victoria's reign.

Hardly an excuse can be made, however, for the artist who drew the " Seal on an Ice-flow " on the 5 cents stamp of 1866 of Newfoundland. The seal has two paws, complete with toes and claws. The artist must have played truant as a schoolboy and perhaps he never visited a zoo, but a glance through a natural history book would have shown him that seals have flippers and not paws. Strangely enough, the same design was used for another stamp several years later, but after many sarcastic protests the Post Office ordered that the stamp should be re-drawn and, in 1880, the seal appeared drawn correctly.

Errors in inscriptions and even in grammar can be found on quite a few stamps. I mentioned the lapse of the Greek post office in issuing a stamp with the portrait of Admiral Codrington, with the caption " Sir Codrington."

We may forgive the Greeks, but the English designer who portrayed Sir Francis Bacon on the 6 cents stamp of Newfoundland of 1910 and described him as "Lord Bacon" should have known better.

That the highest value of North Borneo has the inscription "Ten Dollaps" is probably just the result of absent-mindedness when the lettering was made, but the Russian engraver who produced two Bulgarian stamps in 1885 just did not know whether the Bulgarian coin of "stotinek" was masculine or feminine. He decided to put "edin" and "dva" (one and two) which was masculine and wrong, and the stamps had to be withdrawn and replaced by two using the correct feminine gender—"edna" and "dve," a year later.

Even the Crown Agents, when ordering modern British Colonial designs were not too certain about their grammar and specified the inscription "2½ Penny," where it should have been "2½ Pence." Though realising their blunder, they did not admit it, and subsequent issues were discreetly lettered "2½d."

As I mentioned earlier, overprints have often been misspelled because of the haste in which typesetting and printing has to be done for an emergency issue. Two amusing examples: on the British Guiana 10 cents stamp overprinted in 1899 to be valid as a 2c. value, the printer put in bold letters "TWO GENTS" causing some wry smiles, while another printer when producing a specially overprinted stamp for the wedding of King George II and Queen Lavinia of Tonga antedated their wedding day by ten years, making it "1 JUNE 1889" instead of "1899."

* * *

Stamp designs have caused "international incidents" and have also influenced political decisions. Only a few

ERRORS AND VARIETIES

Errors in designs and flaws caused during printing offer a wide field of study to the more advanced philatelist. Such "varieties" are described in Chapter 8. Our illustrations of two stamps of Fiji show one depicting an unmanned boat and the subsequently issued stamp with the corrected design; a Canadian stamp portraying "the weeping princess," which was caused by a printing flaw, and an Australian stamp which sometimes appeared with a "re-entry" as indicated in the enlarged sketch.

SOME
BRITISH
COMMEMORATIVE
AND
PICTORIAL
STAMPS

years ago, the British government made a strong protest to the government of the Republic of Argentina, after an Argentine 1 peso stamp was issued showing a map of South America with the Falkland Islands appearing as part of Argentina. That South American state had insistently claimed suzerainty over the Falkland Islands which are, of course, a British territory. On the same stamp the frontiers of other South American states were shown, which caused more diplomatic protests by Bolivia and Paraguay, because the Gran Chaco territory (over whose possession the two republics had once gone to war) was drawn as if belonging partly to Argentina. In the end the Argentine post office decided to withdraw the stamp and re-issue it with the South American continent showing no state frontiers at all. The result was that the first stamp is now three times as valuable as the second issue.

The stamp issues of the Free City of Danzig between 1920 and 1939 formed a constant bone of contention between Germany and Poland, and on several occasions nearly led to war until, after Hitler's attack on Poland, the Danzig problem was solved by force of arms.

In many South American revolutions stamps played a "political" part, being overprinted with suitable inscriptions by the temporary victor, only to be once more overprinted when the revolution misfired. Exactly the same happened in 1920 in Hungary. When the short-lived Communist régime of Bela Kun came to power, stamps bearing the inscription "Royal Hungarian Post" were overprinted with "Hungarian Soviet Republic." But after 100 days the Communists were defeated by a right-wing revolution led by Admiral Horthy. There was a shortage of paper and money to issue new stamps, so the new dictator ordered the stocks of the stamps with the Communist overprint to be overprinted once more, this time with a very black picture of a wheat sheaf.

During the last war stamps were "forged" by the Allied Intelligence Service to equip agents parachuted behind the enemy lines. Some of these stamps, bearing the portrait of Marshal Pétain, were hardly distinguishable from the French stamps printed under German occupation, but on the suggestion of General de Gaulle one was printed with a slightly altered design. It showed the familiar portrait of Pétain but behind him was faintly visible the face of Pierre Laval, looking rather Mephistophelean and as if whispering something into Pétain's ear. While Pétain, the famous defender of Verdun in the 1914-18 war, was still respected by the French even though he had come to terms with the Nazis, Laval was hated as a "quisling". The stamp provided good propaganda for the Resistance movement.

Another stamp which caused political trouble was a commemorative of Serbia issued in 1904. It was produced to honour the newly proclaimed King, Peter I, a leader of the revolutionaries who had deposed and assassinated King Alexander I. The design showed the portraits of Peter I and of his ancestor, Kara Georgevich. But the artist, apparently a supporter of the murdered king, worked into the two profiles the outlines of a death mask of Alexander I. The stamp was replaced after a brief currency.

On occasions stamps have offended religious feelings. It happened in France, Germany and Switzerland, when either Catholics or Protestants voiced protests against certain stamp designs. A more serious incident concerned the stamps of Sudan in 1897, when the country was an Anglo-Egyptian condominium and the postal services were controlled by British officials. The stamps showed an Arab postman mounted on a camel and the design was greatly appreciated. Suddenly it was discovered by the Sudanese that the watermark was a cross.

146

Fanatical propaganda was started against the British because they were suspected of a malicious conspiracy to compel the Moslems " to kiss the cross " when putting their lips to the gummed side of the stamps. In fact the watermark was an English rose, though admittedly shaped like a cross. To placate the followers of the Prophet, the postal authorities replaced the stamps with a set of a similar design, but printed on paper showing a Crescent and Star, and peace was restored.

A very similar public outcry occurred in India in 1911, when the attractive set of stamps was issued at the time of King George V's coronation. He was portrayed in the regalia of the Emperor of India, wearing the Imperial Crown and the Grand Collar of the Order of the Star of India. The chain of the order had as pendant a silver-enamelled elephant. For some reason many Muslims believed that the artist had engraved a pig instead of an elephant and, because a pig is regarded as unclean, they took violent offence. It needed many official announcements and the publication of enlarged pictures of the stamps in newspapers and on posters before the hullabaloo died down and the stamps were accepted.

* * *

Criminals have often turned their attention to stamps. Rare stamps can be as valuable as diamonds and gems and they have the additional advantage to a burglar that they can be easily carried off and concealed. Every year newspapers report thefts of valuable collections and only recently one valued at over £50,000 was stolen from a country house in Sussex.

But only one case of a murder committed for a stamp is recorded. In the summer of 1892 a wealthy businessman, M. Gaston Leroux, was found stabbed in his Paris home.

The murder baffled the French police as apparently nothing had been stolen and M. Leroux had no enemies. It seemed that it was a murder without a motive. Then the detective learned that the murdered man was a keen stamp collector. A philatelic expert was asked by the police to check up whether any valuable stamps were missing from his album. After a careful examination of the collection, he reported that only one rare stamp, a 2 cents value of the Hawaii 1851 " Missionary " issue appeared to have been taken out of one of the albums. The stamp was then valued at about £200—to-day it is catalogued at £5,000— and was one of the rarest in M. Leroux' collection. The police established that one of the victim's philatelic friends, Hector Girou, had visited him on the day of the murder. Girou was interrogated but indignantly denied being the killer. However, when his own collection was inspected, the missing stamp was found and the philatelic expert declared that it had been only quite recently mounted on the album leaf. Girou finally made a full confession. He said he had for years coveted the possession of this stamp, the only value which was missing from his set of the first Hawaii issue. When Leroux refused to sell it to him, he decided to murder his friend. Girou was sentenced to death and died under the guillotine.

Whodunits, films, stage, radio and television plays have been written around stamps, with eccentric collectors, villains, spies and killers involved in blood-curdling robberies, murders and intrigues, but the Leroux case was the only murder case with a philatelic motive that happened in real life.

However, one of the most daring frauds ever perpetrated in Britain was real enough. It is known as the " Great Stock Exchange Stamp Forgery." In the 1870's, when the telephone service was not yet introduced, the brokers at the London Stock Exchange communicated with their clients by telegram. Many hundreds, sometimes thousands, of telegrams were sent every day from the telegraph office in the Stock Exchange Building. Most of these telegrams were quite short, mentioning the names of a consol, share, or bond and the latest price, and the uniform charge was 1 shilling. The fee was paid in stamps and almost exclusively the 1s. green of the 1865-67 design with the head of Queen Victoria was used.

Telegram forms are destroyed some time after delivery, and in 1896 there was a " leakage " when bales of old forms were sent to a paper mill for pulping. An employee of the post office took some of these old forms, thinking that they were of no value anyway, and they were subsequently acquired by the well-known stamp dealer, Mr. Charles Nissen. Examining the 1s. stamps, the dealer discovered that all of them were forgeries, printed on paper without a watermark. He immediately notified the G.P.O. and a lengthy investigation began. It was found that, seemingly for two years, between 1870 and 1872, all shilling stamps used at the Stock Exchange had been forgeries. Apparently a " master-mind " in complicity with a dishonest post office clerk had printed and supplied the forgeries, which were then sold at the proper face value to the stockbrokers' clerks who dispatched the telegrams. Probably many thousands of these forgeries were thus sold to the detriment of the postal authority. The culprits, who must have made a fortune, were never discovered, because the existence of these forgeries was established only a quarter of a century after the crime. Ironically, though the G.P.O. had been the victim of a fraud on a grand scale, these forgeries have been eagerly sought after ever since by specialists of Great Britain.

A crime of a very different kind was committed just before the outbreak of the last war—by ants! The last " white " Rajah of Sarawak, Sir Charles Vyner Brooke, was an ardent stamp collector. When he returned to his palace from a visit to England, he had a terrible surprise. Termites had invaded the cupboards in which his stamp albums were kept and had eaten, page by page and from cover to cover, thousands of his valuable stamps. The Rajah was so disgusted that he decided to give up collecting, realising that in the tropical climate of his kingdom in North Borneo it was too risky a hobby. What he could salvage of his collection was finally auctioned in London.

There are strange stories galore connected with stamps and stamp collecting and they add interest, sometimes perhaps morbid or scurrilous, to the other ramifications of the hobby.

CHAPTER 14

Friendly Philately

A well-known philatelist, who was also a distinguished London surgeon, summed up his interest in stamp collecting by saying: " Philately gave me much amusement, much knowledge and, above all, many friendships."

It is an undisputed fact that stamp collectors are friendly people. It may be that, because they have found enjoyment in their hobby, they delight in conveying the charms of this pursuit to others. I have been a member of many societies and clubs in my lifetime: academic, professional, regimental, social and sporting. My considered opinion is that nowhere have I encountered happier, more friendly and helpful men and women than among stamp collectors and members of philatelic clubs. Doctors and psychiatrists recommend stamp collecting as a hobby, because they find that the study of stamps brings the relaxation which we need to recover from the constant stress and strain of our everyday life.

I seriously urge every beginner to join a local philatelic society, of which there are more than 200 in Britain. Most public libraries will supply the address of the honorary secretary to whom application for membership can be made. Admission is informal, though a reference will be requested. The annual subscription is quite modest, rarely more than 10 shillings.

On his very first visit to a meeting the newcomer will be made welcome and get all the assistance and advice he wants. In every philatelic society there are several " old hands," experienced, knowledgeable and often distinguished philatelists, who will take a delight in guiding the newcomer. In London there are philatelic societies in every district and also several " specialist societies " and " study circles " whose members are devoted to the collecting of stamps of a particular country or a particular field. Thus, there are study groups for Australia, Canada, and other Commonwealth countries, for France, Switzerland, Holland, Ireland, Russia, Poland, Egypt, China and other foreign countries, for Postal History, Airmails, Seaposts, Thematic Collecting and so on.

Then there are the large national organisations such as the British Philatelic Association and the National Philatelic Society. These publish their own well-edited and illustrated journals and provide many facilities for their members, including library service, expertising, etc. The Royal Philatelic Society is the " club " of the advanced specialists and experts and admission is by election.

But even without aspiring too high at first, the beginner will do very well in his local society, whether it is in one of the twenty-six in Greater London or at Arbroath, Brynmawr, Devizes, Morecambe, Sittingbourne, Tewkesbury and two hundred other towns from John o' Groats to Land's End, because even the smallest society holds regular monthly meetings with displays of members' collections, lectures, discussions, exchange evenings, club auctions and socials, and most have good libraries and run an Exchange Packet.

The Exchange Packet service is particularly useful for the beginner. It is organised as follows: members are invited to send to the Secretary (or Exchange Packet Superintendent) a number of booklets (available from him) in which they mount their duplicates or stamps they desire to dispose of. Each stamp is priced at " retail price," that is at a price which is lower than the catalogue quotation. For the convenience of members the catalogue number should be written above the stamp and any useful remark added, if the stamp is a variety, a special shade, etc. These booklets, each with the name of the " contributor " on the cover, are assembled into " packets " of 20 or more and sent in a box by the Secretary to all members of the society in rotation, as a rule once monthly. The packet is insured against loss or damage. The member who receives it is allowed to keep it for 48 hours, picks out any stamps he wants and then, after having packed and sealed it carefully, forwards the box to another member, according to the enclosed " posting list." When all members on the list have received the packet, the last named member returns it to the Secretary. In the meantime every member who has bought stamps from the booklets sends to the Secretary his remittance with a " notification form " which is enclosed in the box for every member. The Secretary checks the sales and returns the booklets to the contributors, with the remittance for their sales, after deducting a small commission (as a rule 10%) for the expenses incurred by the society.

It is buying and selling rather than " exchanging " stamps, but cashless transactions would be impracticable by mail and this procedure works extremely well. Cashless exchange (when stamps change hands at catalogue quotations or agreed valuation) take place in some societies at club meetings, to which members bring their duplicates.

There exist also a number of professional " Exchange Clubs," run by dealers much on the same lines. Obviously, the prices of the stamps offered by them will be somewhat higher; the organisers have to cover their overheads and want to make a modest profit. Addresses of reputable Exchange Clubs can be gleaned from their advertisements in philatelic journals.

The majority of the societies are affiliated to the Philatelic Congress of Great Britain, which assembles every year (since 1909) in one of the large cities or seaside resorts for a week's session, and also to the British Philatelic Association. All committee members such as chairmen, secretaries, treasurers, etc. are honorary officers and give much of their leisure time to their clubs for the love of the hobby and, alas, are often out of pocket.

Apart from the G.P.O.'s monthly *Philatelic Bulletin*, already mentioned, several excellent philatelic periodicals are published in Britain: *Stamp Collecting* (weekly), *The Philatelic Magazine* (fortnightly), and *Stamp Magazine* (monthly) being the leading ones. Several dealers also publish magazines, for instance Stanley Gibbons Ltd. who publish *Gibbons Stamp Monthly*. Together with many excellent articles this contains supplements to all Gibbons' catalogues. The small outlay for an annual subscription for one or several of these journals will be quickly repaid. Even if the beginner finds that some of the articles are a little above his head, dealing perhaps with one issue of a country, or containing a discourse about some rare stamps, there is always a wealth of general information included and all the magazines cater for beginners as well as for advanced collectors. These periodicals also publish descriptions and illustrations of new issues of all countries, keeping the collector up to date.

Under the patronage of the great societies, such as the Royal or the B.P.A. (British Philatelic Association) and the National Philatelic Society, next to the Royal, Britain's oldest general society with some 10,000 members, and with the co-operation of the Philatelic Traders Society, many stamp exhibitions have been organised since 1890 in Britain. Apart from the annual National Stamp Exhibition—"Stampex"—that is normally held in March or April, it has become customary to organise a major International Stamp Exhibition every 10 years. In 1960 it took place at the Festival Hall; and in 1970, under the title—

" Philympia "—it is again being held in London, at Olympia from 18-26 September, 1970. With accommodation for approximately 3,600 display frames in the competitive section, there is room enough for all the major collections to be represented.

The British G.P.O. are showing the biggest display they have ever provided at any exhibition: its theme is " The Penny Black " and it includes many historical items never before exhibited. Her Majesty the Queen has also given permission for the display of a number of rare items from the Royal Collection.

Such an exhibition provides a unique opportunity to examine closely pages from some of the finest British and foreign collections.

For the beginner as well as the advanced philatelist a visit to an exhibition is a thrilling and advantageous event. There he can inspect the great philatelic treasures, see stamps which, though he may never possess them, will fire his enthusiasm for further study. The beginner will pick up many hints for the arrangement and writing-up of his own collection and see how more experienced collectors cope with the many problems which still puzzle him.

Also very important to the stamp collector are the regular stamp auctions which take place mainly in London, but also from time to time in many cities and towns of the British Isles. I should like to advise the beginner to attend a few auctions, even if he does not intend to make any bids at first. The lots offered can be inspected beforehand in the auctioneer's showrooms and here again the beginner can enlarge his knowledge.

In this country there is, of course, now the National Postal Museum and when spending a holiday abroad it is a good idea to visit the foreign postal museums, particularly those in Paris, Berne and Munich which have marvellous displays, and also to contact a local philatelic society. As in

Britain there are such societies in many towns and resorts abroad, and one will find a welcome as warm and friendly as that extended by British collectors. Though language difficulties may intervene, there will always be somebody present who speaks or understands English. Spending an evening or a Sunday afternoon among French, Italian, Swiss, German or Scandinavian collectors will add to the pleasures of a holiday and, more likely than not, a friendship will be made that will endure. Many a friendship has been founded in this way. The " stranger " was invited to the home of the new-won friend and sometimes even asked to spend his next holiday with him and his family. Philately and philatelists have contributed much to the understanding between men and women and young people of many races and tongues and have probably contributed more to international peace and goodwill than some of the more well-publicised efforts of statesmen and diplomats.

Index

*The asterisked page numbers * refer to illustrations*